"I personally have benefited in countless ways from the FOCUSed15 Bible study method. I am grateful to Katie for her work and for bringing me back to Jesus over and over again in each of these studies. Everyday Peace *was a safe harbor for me in the middle of life's storms. As with every other book in the series, Katie Orr helps make Bible study easy, helpful, and soul-enriching."*

—JESSICA THOMPSON, author Everyday Grace and coauthor of Give Them Grace

"We all want to spend time studying the Bible and growing our relationship with Jesus. But then life gets busy and we end up wondering what happened to our good intentions. Katie Orr understands this, and through the FOCUSed15 Bible study method, she's provided a practical and inspirational solution. You'll have the tools you need to do what your heart truly desires."

—HOLLY GERTH, best-selling author and cofounder of DaySpring's (in)courage blog

"Katie Orr has a passion for Scripture and for women to know Scripture. This passion shows in her FOCUSed15 Bible study method, which she uses to lead women through books of the Bible and topical doctrinal studies. She proves that inductive Bible study doesn't have to be complicated, but can be deeply impactful and fruitful."

—CHRISTINE HOOVER, author of From Good to Grace and The Church Planting Wife

"The FOCUSed15 Bible study method gives women an opportunity to learn the tools of inductive Bible Study in bite-sized chunks. Perfect for anyone who is committed to studying the Word in this time-crunched culture!"

—ANDREA BUCZYNSKI, vice president of global leadership development/ human resources for Cru

"The Scriptures are like jewels. When you look from different angles they glimmer in beautiful and unexpected ways. The FOCUSed15 Bible study method gives a fresh way to examine and enjoy the most precious words on earth. Katie Orr's zeal for God's Word is contagious and may forever change the way you engage the Bible."

—JESSE LANE, vice president of connections at Seed Company

"Katie Orr has both the unique ability to make deep, meaningful Bible study doable for others and a passion for helping women love God more through the study of His Word. Through her Bible studies, Katie teaches others how to methodically grasp and absorb biblical theology in digestible bite-sized chunks. Her distinct and approachable gift of leading others through Scripture gives those with a desire to dive into God's Word a wonderful opportunity to both understand and apply deep biblical truths in their every day."

—CHRYSTAL EVANS HURST, coauthor of *Kingdom Woman*

"Katie Orr is a woman captivated by the Word and person of God. Her heart beats to uncover the truth of Christ for herself and to make those hard-won truths accessible to others. They say that the mark of a good leader is that her work will point people toward God more than herself, and if that's true, then Katie Orr is exactly the kind of leader I personally want to follow."

—LOGAN WOLFRAM, author of *Curious Faith* and executive director and host of Allume

"Everywhere I go women are searching for discipleship tools, either for themselves or for those they are discipling. Katie Orr has delivered up a fresh, substantive tool to accomplish both. FOCUSed15 is a serious study method that is possible even for those with demanding responsibilities. This material will fit in a variety of settings and for women everywhere on their spiritual journey."

—KATHY FERGUSON LITTON, national consultant for ministry to pastors' wives, North American Mission Board

"Katie Orr brings a unique and productive method of studying Scripture to the world of Bible studies. I enthusiastically encourage women to explore this effective and enjoyable method of Bible study!"

—SUZIE HAWKINS, author and longtime member of Southern Baptist Convention Pastors' Wives, wife of O. S. Hawkins

"Katie Orr has designed devotional material for the busy woman in mind—a focused 15 minutes a day that leads the reader to encounter the biblical text with guidance that reinforces solid principles of biblical interpretation and helpful application that makes God's Word come alive in our daily choices."

—TREVIN WAX, managing editor of The Gospel Project, LifeWay Christian Resources

Other books in the

FOCUSed15 Bible study series:

EVERYDAY **faith***:*
Drawing Near to His Presence

EVERYDAY **hope***:*
Holding Fast to His Promise

EVERYDAY **love***:*
Bearing Witness to His Purpose

EVERYDAY

Standing Firm
in His Provision

KATIE ORR

NEW HOPE®
PUBLISHERS
Gospel-Centered. Missions-Driven.

BIRMINGHAM, ALABAMA

New Hope® Publishers
PO Box 12065
Birmingham, AL 35202-2065
NewHopePublishers.com
New Hope Publishers is a division of WMU®.

Library of Congress Cataloging-in-Publication Data
Names: Orr, Katie, 1978- author.
Title: Everyday peace : standing firm in his provision / Katie Orr.
Description: Birmingham, AL : New Hope Publishers, 2016.
Identifiers: LCCN 2016019902 | ISBN 9781625915061 (sc)
Subjects: LCSH: Peace--Biblical teaching. | Bible. Philippians, IV--Textbooks.
Classification: LCC BS2705.6.P5 O77 2016 | DDC 248.8/6--dc23 LC record available at https://lccn.loc.gov/2016019902

ISBN-13: 978-1-62591-506-1

N174105 • 0916 • 3M1

Dedication

To my siblings.

Sarah and Nathan, I'm so proud of all that
both of you have become. You are full of integrity,
hard work, and love for others. I love you.

James, we miss you. Always.

Table of Contents

Introduction

→ Lord, you establish peace for us. —Isaiah 26:12 NIV ←

MY EVERYDAY PEACE is easily stolen. It only takes a simple glance at the latest world news or my mounting to-do list for uncertainty and restlessness to rise up and overwhelm my heart with anxiety. Yet another look at the success and joys of those around me can lure my soul into a never-ending longing for the possessions, personality traits, and positions in life I do not have. Just one encounter with a difficult person or a sticky exchange can quickly rob my days of peace.

Everyday peace is something I have to fight for.

I expect you might be knee-deep in this fight as well. In fact, you might feel as if you are battered and bruised, defeated by the thieves of peace. Anxiety fills your moments. Dissension defines your relationships. Discontentment rules your days.

If you find yourself lacking peace, be encouraged. You are not alone. In fact, the minute I began writing this Bible study, my anxiety levels seemed to triple, my lack of contentment incredibly evident, and (after years of peace-filled friendships) multiple relational wild-fires popped up out of nowhere. Opportunities to engage in the fight for everyday peace were abundant.

As we'll see in our study together, everyday peace is ushered in or shut out of our lives through the choices we make. Anxiety, dissension, and discontentment stare us in the face daily (if not hourly!) and these peace-robbers will continue to trail us and attempt to invade our hearts as long as we live on this sin-stained earth. Though we cannot always avoid these enemies of peace, we do have a choice when we encounter them. And the actions needed to fight for peace may not be what you think.

As you journey through this study, I'm praying you'll have eyes to see (though it may seem distant and maybe even impossible) that everyday peace can be cultivated. Not by managing your emotions or self-helping your way to a status of serenity. Everyday peace is within reach because it has been granted to us by our faithful, generous God. He has fought and won the battle for peace. Our job is to stand firm in the provision He's already given us.

Through the presence of God, the strength of the Spirit, and the example of Christ, our every moment can be saturated with the peace that surpasses understanding. He is working in and around you to establish this promised peace for you. God's plan for you is everyday peace. Over these next four weeks, pray for it. Work toward it. He will provide.

{God, bring Your peace into my moments. I long to experience the peace that passes all understanding in my everyday life. I confess my need for you to reveal to me the role I play in everyday peace. Holy Spirit, I open every nook and cranny of my heart and mind for You to carefully inspect, gently correct, and powerfully transform.}

The Need for Focus

IF THIS IS your first FOCUSed15 study, you'll want to carefully read through the following introduction and study method instructions. After that, I'll see you on Day 1!

It's hard to focus.

In a world filled with continual demands for my attention, I struggle to keep a train of thought. Tasks I need to do. Appointments I need to remember. Projects I need to complete.

Yeah, it's hard to focus.

Without a good focus for my days, I wander. I lack the ability to choose well and to avoid the tyranny of the urgent. Without focus, days become a blur—tossed back and forth between the pressing and the enticing.

Why Focus Matters

I felt pretty lost during my first attempts at spending time with God in the Bible. After a few weeks of wandering around the Psalms and flipping through the New Testament, I realized I had no clue what I was doing.

It felt like a pretty big waste of time.

I knew the Bible was full of life-changing truths and life-giving promises, but I needed to learn how to focus on the details to see all that Scripture held for me.

In the medical world, we depend on the microscope. Even with all the fancy machines that can give test results in seconds, the microscope has yet to become obsolete. Some things can only be discovered through the lens of the scope.

What looks like nothing to the naked eye is actually teeming with life-threatening bacteria. Even under the microscope they may not be seen at first glance. But with the smallest adjustment of the focus, the blurry cloud of the field in view is brought into focus and the finest details are revealed.

And those details matter.

You need a microscope to make a diagnosis, but the microscope itself doesn't make the discoveries. It takes a trained eye to distinguish between cells. The average person may be able to figure out how to use the microscope to find a cell and get it in focus, but without training, the beginner will not know the clinical significance of what is seen.

Similarly, when we approach God's Word, we must learn to focus on what we see and develop a trained eye to know its significance.

Ready for More

I grew up in a shallow Christian culture. Don't do drugs. Don't have sex. Don't tell lies. Read your Bible. Be a light—sold-out for Jesus. This was the sum of being a good Christian, or so I thought.

Now, I'm your typical firstborn list-checker, so the do's and don'ts worked for me . . . for a while. But as I got older and the temptations of the don'ts became more enticing, I began to wonder if this Christianity thing was worth it.

Is this really what people spend their lives chasing? Seems tiring—and ultimately worthless.

Yet, God was drawing my heart—I could undeniably feel it—but I knew I was missing something. I thought I'd check out this reading-the-Bible thing. Sure, I had read a devotional or two and knew all the Bible stories, but I didn't feel I knew God Himself.

A bit nervous, I drove to the local bookstore to buy my first really nice Bible. I excitedly drove back home, and headed straight to my room, opened up my leather-bound beauty and began to read . . .

. . . and nothing happened.

I'm not quite sure what I was expecting, but it sure wasn't confusion and frustration. I decided to give it another try the next day and still heard nothing. I had no clue what I was reading.

In all my years of storing up the do's and don'ts in my how-to-be-a-good-Christian box, I never caught a how or why.

For years I stumbled through my black leather Bible with very little learned on the other side of it all. Yet, God was faithful to lead and speak, and I fully believe that He can and does speak to us through His Word, even if we are as clueless as I was.

However, I also believe that God's Word is meant to be a great catalyst in our growth, and as we pursue how to better know God through His Word, we will experience Him in deeper ways.

You and I need a healthy, rich diet of God's Word in order to grow. And as we read, study, and learn to digest the Bible, we move toward becoming more like Christ. When we pursue the nearness of God, the don'ts become lackluster compared to the life-giving promises of His Word.

A FOCUSed 15 Minutes

Over time, I learned how to use incredible Bible study tools that took my time with God in His Word to a deeper level. Yet with each method, Bible study seemed to take more and more time. Certain seasons of life allow for a leisurely time in the Bible; my experience has proven that most of my days don't.

As much as I would love to find a comfy chair in my favorite local coffee shop and study God's Word for hours, it is just not often possible. I'm lucky if I can get a decent breakfast in every morning before my day starts rolling. Distractions and demands abound, and many days I have not even tried to study my Bible because I just didn't have what it would take, time-wise, to get much out of it.

Until I learned to focus.

Even the busiest Christians can learn to focus and train their eyes to discover the life-changing truths held in Scripture. No incredibly long "quiet times" or seminary degree required.

All it takes is a focused 15 minutes.

The method I will walk you through consists of 15 minutes, five days a week. We will focus on the same set of verses over the course of a week, and each day of that week we will look at the passage with a different lens to gather new insights along the way.

Two Ultimate Goals

My prayer for you as we dive into the Bible is twofold. First, I want to work myself out of a job. I want you to walk away from this study a bit more confident in your ability to focus on the transformational truths of Scripture on your own.

Second, I hope you will encounter our God in a deep and meaningful way through these focused 15 minutes. The most important thing about us is what we believe about God, and my prayer is that you will more accurately understand the truths about who He is through your own study of Scripture. As you get to know our glorious God better and better each day, I think you'll see your actions and attitudes are forever changed—because of who He is.

What You'll Need

A pen to record your study notes and a journal for additional notes and any bonus study work you choose to do.

A Bible. If you don't have one, I recommend investing in a good study Bible. Visit my resources page at KatieOrr.me for solid study Bible suggestions.

Both a Greek interlinear Bible and Greek lexicon. There are in-print and free online versions for both. Check out my resources page for links.

A Few Important Notes

This is only one method. This approach is my attempt at distilling down how I enjoy spending time in God's Word. There are other great methods I use from time to time. Take what you can from this method and use what works for you; make it your own.

Fifteen minutes is just the starting point. Some of us are in a stage of life where we'll take 15 minutes whenever we can get it. Others may be able to carve out more time. I will give you suggestions for how to shorten or lengthen the study as needed. I think you will find yourself looking up at the clock and realizing you've accomplished a lot in a short amount of time.

Using online study tools will be of great help. You can certainly do this study without getting online; however, you will expedite many of the processes by utilizing the powerful—and free—online tools I suggest throughout our time together. I totally get that being online while trying to connect with God has its distracting challenges. Do what works for you. There is no "right" way to do this study. The only way to "fail" is to stop meeting with God.

Resist the urge to consult commentaries and study Bible notes right away. I am thankful for all the resources we have at our fingertips, but oftentimes devotionals, study Bibles, and the latest, greatest Bible teacher can be a crutch that keeps us from learning how to walk intimately with God on our own. While I do believe there is only one true meaning of each verse, God has a personalized word to speak to each of us through this study. Receiving big news from a loved one in a deliberate and personalized way means so much more to us than receiving the news third-hand, and when the Holy

Spirit reveals a message to our hearts through God's Word, it will be something we hold to much more closely than someone else's experience of God. If at the end of the week, you are still unsure of the meaning of the passage, you can then look through commentaries.

For a list of my favorite online and print resources, including Greek study tools, commentaries, cross-referencing tools, and study Bibles, check out my resources page at KatieOrr.me.

How to FOCUS

OVER THE NEXT four weeks we will study peace together using the FOCUSed15 study method. Think of me as your Bible coach. I will point you to the goal, give you what you need, and cheer you on—but you'll be the one doing the work.

The FOCUSed15 method may be different from other studies you've completed. We're focusing on quality, not quantity. The goal is not to see how quickly we can get through each verse, but how deeply we can go into each verse and find everything we can about the peace portrayed. This is how we can go deeper, in as little as 15 minutes a day, by looking at the same passage over the course of several days, each day using a new lens to view it. We're not trying to get everything we can out of the passage the first time we sit in front of it. Instead, we'll come back to it again and again, peeling back each layer, 15 minutes at a time.

Here is where we're headed:

- » **Week 1**—*How Do I Find Everyday Peace?*

- » **Week 2**—*Peace in My Everyday Stress: FOCUSing on Philippians 4:4–9*

- » **Week 3**—*Peace in Any Circumstance: FOCUSing on Philippians 4:10–13*

- » **Week 4**—*Peace in Dissension: FOCUSing on Philippians 4:1–3*

The FOCUSed15 Bible Study Method

For me, high school history homework typically consisted of answering a set of questions at the end of the chapter. I quickly found that the best use of my time was to take each question, one at a time, and skim through the chapter with the question in mind. So, if the question was about Constantine, I would read the chapter wearing my "Constantine Glasses." All I looked for were facts about Constantine.

Little did I know then, this "glasses" method would become my favorite way to study God's Word. The FOCUSed15 method is essentially changing to a new pair of glasses with each read, using a different focus than the read before. Together, we will study one passage for five days, each day using a different part of the FOCUSed15 method.

- » **Day 1**—*Foundation: Enjoy Every Word*
- » **Day 2**—*Observation: Look at the Details*
- » **Day 3**—*Clarification: Uncover the Original Meaning*
- » **Day 4**—*Utilization: Discover the Connections*
- » **Day 5**—*Summation: Respond to God's Word*

For each day in our study, I will guide you through a different lens of the FOCUSed15 study method, designed to be completed in as little as 15 minutes a day. There are also bonus study ideas with every day, providing ways to spend more time and dig even deeper if you can. We'll pray together each day, declaring our dependence on the Spirit of God to open the eyes of our hearts to the truths in God's Word.

Foundation—Enjoy Every Word

Many of us are conditioned to read through Scripture quickly and are often left having no idea what we just read. So, to kick off our studies, we will write out our verses. Nothing too fancy, but an incredibly efficient way to slow down and pay attention to each word on the page.

Observation—Look at the Details

With our foundation work behind us, we'll spend the next day looking for truths in God's Word. This is a powerful use of our time; we cannot rightly apply the Bible to our lives if we do not accurately see what is there. Observation is simply noting what we see by asking ourselves a set of questions. We're not yet trying to figure out what it means, we are simply beginning an assessment. I will guide you along the way as we look for specific truths like, "What does this passage say is true about peace?"

Clarification—Uncover the Original Meaning

This is going to be fun. We'll take a peek at the original language of the verses. Our three passages are in the New Testament, so we'll look up the original Greek they were written in. To do this we'll follow three simple steps:

Step 1: DECIDE which word you would like to study.

In this step, we will look for any repeated words or keywords words to look up, choose one, and learn more about it.

Step 2: DISCOVER that word as it was originally written.

Next, using an interlinear Bible, we'll find the original Greek word for the English word we chose in Step 1.

Step 3: DEFINE that word.

Finally, we will learn about the full meaning of each Greek word using a Greek lexicon, which is very much like a dictionary. We'll walk through an example together each week. You can also bookmark How to Do a Greek Word Study in the appendix for your reference throughout the study.

Utilization—Discover the Connections

The infallible rule of interpretation of Scripture is the Scripture itself: and therefore, when there is a question about the true and full sense of any Scripture . . . it must be searched and known by other places that speak more clearly.

—THE WESTMINSTER CONFESSION OF FAITH

Ever notice the little numbers and letters inserted in your study Bible? Most have them. The numbers are footnotes, helpful bits of information about the original text. The little letters are cross-references and important tools for study.

Cross-references do just that, referencing across the Bible where the word or phrase is used in other passages. They may also refer to a historical event or prophecy significant to the verse you are studying.

Together, we will follow a few of the cross-references for each of our passages, as they will often lead us to a better understanding of the main teaching of our verses. If your Bible doesn't have cross-references, no worries! I will provide verses for you to look up, and refer you to online tools for bonus studies.

Summation—Respond to God's Word

A respectable acquaintance with the opinions of the giants of the past, might have saved many an erratic thinker from wild interpretations and outrageous inferences.

—CHARLES SPURGEON

This is when we begin to answer the question, "How should this passage affect me?" To understand this we will take three actions:

1. Identify—Find the main idea of the passage.

With a robust study of our passage accomplished, we can now do the work of interpretation. Interpretation is simply figuring out what it all means. This is oftentimes difficult to do. However, if we keep in mind the context and make good observations of the text, a solid interpretation will typically result.

This is when we will finally consult our study Bibles and commentaries! Commentaries are invaluable tools when interpreting Scripture. They are available on the entire Bible, as well as volumes on just one book of the Bible. For a list of free online commentaries, as well as in-print investments, check out KatieOrr.me/Resources.

2. Modify—Evaluate my beliefs in light of the main idea.

Once we have figured out what the passage means, we can now apply the passage to our lives. Many tend to look at application as simply finding something to change in their actions. Much in the Bible will certainly lead us to lifestyle changes, but there is another category of application that we often miss: what we believe.

We must learn to see the character of God in what we study and ask ourselves how our view of Him lines up with what we see. Of course it is helpful to look for do's and don'ts to follow, but without an ever-growing knowledge of who God is, the commands become burdensome.

3. Glorify—Align my life to reflect the truth of God's Word.

When we see God for the glorious, grace-filled Savior He is, the natural response is worship; the do's and don'ts become a joy as they become a way to honor the One we love with our lives. Worship is true application.

All of This . . . in 15 Minutes?

Yes, I know this seems like a lot of ground to cover. Don't worry! I will be here to walk you through each day. Remember, instead of trying to go as fast as we can through a passage, we are going to take it slow and intentionally. We'll look at one passage for an entire week, and apply one part of the method to the passage each day.

The Cheat Sheet

At the end of most days' studies, I've included a "cheat sheet." While trying to complete a Bible study, I've often been paralyzed with wondering, "Am I doing this the right way?" The cheat sheet is there for you to use as a reference point. It is not a list of correct answers, however, and is meant instead to provide just a little bit of guidance here and there to let you know you are on the right track.

There are also several references in the appendix you may want to consult throughout our time together. If you are new to Bible study, you might consider spending a day to read through the appendices before beginning your study. I hope those pages will be of great help to you.

A Note to the Overwhelmed

Bible study is not a competition or something to achieve. It is a way of communicating with our magnificent God. If you have little time or mental capacity (I've been there, moms with little ones!), ignore the bonus study ideas and enjoy what you can. Keep moving through the study each day, and know that you have taken a step of obedience to meet with God in His Word. Other seasons of life will allow for longer, deeper study. For now, embrace these precious moments in the Word and remember that Jesus is your righteousness. When God looks at you—overwhelmed and burned-out though you are—He sees the faithful obedience and perfection of Christ on your behalf, and He is pleased. Rest in that today, weary one.

HOW DO I FIND

Everyday Peace?

Our Source of Peace

Now may the Lord of peace himself give you peace at all times in every way.
—2 Thessalonians 3:16

I'M, BY NATURE, a planner. Over a decade ago, my husband Chris and I spent six weeks in Asia with a team of students. Preparations began months prior, especially since we had a baby with us who was only seven months old when we began the trip. Not knowing what would be available to us, I planned out all the baby items (especially diapers!) we would need to bring with us to cover our time there. The planning and packing served us well and we spent a mostly smooth six weeks living on campus in a large city with baby Kenneth in tow.

What we hadn't planned for is all we would bring home to America. Shopping in China was oh-so-much fun. We designed pearl necklaces at the Pearl Market in Beijing, selected silk and moleskin for quilted throws at the local fabric market, ordered custom scrolls, and had our favorite shirts and pants recreated by a talented seamstress. The prices for these items were unheard of in America, so we stocked up on gifts for Christmas and birthdays for the upcoming year. All this shopping led us to one last inevitable purchase before we could leave for home: another suitcase. After spending the day hopping in and out of taxis, we finally found the suitcase market and picked out a brand name, sturdy-looking, bright-red rolling suitcase. We carried it back to our apartment and packed it full with our acquisitions from the summer.

When it was time to depart and begin our trek home, I grasped the retracting handle and headed to our taxi. That's where my troubles began. The handle came with me, but the rest of the suitcase remained on the porch of our apartment. We managed to shove the handle back into the suitcase, hoping for it to stick. It did, long enough for me to roll the suitcase five feet ahead where the wheels proceeded to fall off. Along the rest of our journey, the zipper began to unravel from the case, and the branding decal fell off, too. The luggage, most certainly, was a fake. This counterfeit suitcase, which had promised to provide structure and ease of use for decades to come, wasn't even going to give us what we needed for our 24-hour trip home. What looked like a quality piece of luggage—the real deal—proved to be a quickly disassembling piece of garbage.

My soul craves peace. However, I often buy into the lie that peace can be purchased by an afternoon of solitude or a weekend at the beach. Peace is not a state of mind, a cease-fire, or a serene setting. Anything or anyone who promises peace is a counterfeit. True and lasting soul-level peace is found only in a Person: the God of all peace.

1. Take a moment to begin your study in prayer. Use the space below to journal a prayer, asking the Holy Spirit to open your eyes to the reality about peace. Commit these next four weeks of study to God.

Before we move into our inductive (verse-by-verse) study of our three passages on peace, we need to get a big picture of how the Bible defines peace. To start our journey toward a better under-standing of peace, let's read a few verses while asking the question, "Where does peace come from?"

2. Start first with writing out Romans 15:33 below.

3. According to this verse, where does peace come from?

4. Next, write out the first sentence of 1 Corinthians 14:33.

5. Note, in the chart below, what is true of God and what is not true of God, according to the first sentence of 1 Corinthians 14:33.

True of God	NOT True of God

God is referred to as "the God of peace" over and over again in Scripture. Fifteen of the biblical epistles (the technical term for letters written to churches, such as Philippians, Galatians, Ephesians, etc.) give a greeting to their beloved church members, which includes some version of the phrase "peace from God." These, alongside other verses teaching on peace, make a strong case from the New Testament of where peace originates. True and lasting peace comes from God alone.

6. Lastly, move back to the Old Testament to look up Isaiah 9:6. This is a prophecy given of the Christ child to come, which was fulfilled in the birth of Jesus. Read the verse, then list all of the names given for the promised child.

The Almighty God of the Bible is the only source of true peace. He alone has the power to put an end to waging wars and family feuds. Our God can bring a peace to our souls that no treaty or truce can provide. Every anxious thought, every relational rift, and every restless desire can be captured and calmed through the presence and provision of Jesus, the Prince of Peace.

> *{God, I am so thankful You are a God of peace. Amidst this world of confusion and dissension, You are a sure and steady rock I can cling to. When the troubles of my day threaten to steal my joy, help me keep my eyes on You today, my God of peace.}*

Bonus Study

Read and write out the first chapter of Philippians. If you have additional time, create three columns in your journal: *Truths, Promises, Commands.* As you read Philippians 1, note any words or phrases that fit into each category.

Cheat Sheet

3. According to this verse, where does peace come from?

God

5. Note, in the chart below, what is true of God and what is not true of God, according to the first sentence of 1 Corinthians 14:33.

True of God	NOT True of God
God of Peace	God of Confusion

Our Way to Peace

Jesus said to him, "I am the way, and the truth, and the life. No one comes to the Father except through me."—John 14:6

GROWING UP IN southern California, I frequented Disneyland as a child. I have so many fond memories of entering Main Street filled with excitement and rushing to be first in line for Big Thunder Mountain. A few years ago, while we were down in Florida visiting for Christmas, my husband's grandma surprised our kids with tickets to the Magic Kingdom. So a few days after Christmas, we stuffed our backpack with snacks and sunscreen, donned our coordinating Disney duds, and hit the park pavement. As did the rest of the world's tourists. The parking lot shut down by 10 a.m. All day long, the walkways were a continuum of people. Everywhere.

We were shoulder to shoulder with the masses all day long. And the wait times were horrendous. Since my oldest was finally big enough to ride Space Mountain, a fast-paced indoor roller coaster, we continually checked line times, looking for a chance to jump in without having to wait hours, but to no avail. Late in the evening, as we watched Anna and Elsa turn the castle into a frozen fortress, surrounded by thousands of others also watching the show, it dawned on us that the lines must now be short! We checked our Disney iPhone app, and indeed, the line was shorter than it had been all day. We immediately began the quick route east to Tomorrowland from Liberty Square.

Unfortunately, every 20 yards or so, there was a detour. The straight path to Space Mountain was blocked off for the Main Street parade, and we were diverted south again and again, turning what should have been a quick walk to the "short" 45-minute wait into one of the longest treks of my life: two very tired adults attempting to cajole a faster pace from three also tired children (who have been on their feet all day and are now up way past their bedtime), only to be frustrated with turn after unnecessary turn, driving us farther and farther away from our destination. When we finally made it to Space Mountain, the original wait projection had tripled.

Looking back on the evening, if we had chosen to go north from Liberty Square, back toward the Haunted House and then southeast through Fantasyland, we would have sailed through to Tomorrowland and the short Space Mountain line. For that evening, at that moment, there was only one way to our goal. Though there were other routes we tried, only one would have delivered.

Many spend their lives trying to get to God taking the wrong route. Through works, good deeds, and self-righteousness, they attempt to enter into peace with God through a never-ending path that only frustrates and detours. Seeking forgiveness from God, right standing before Him, and eternal security in His presence is a worthwhile pursuit. All of these usher the peace that surpasses understanding into the depths of our souls. It is this we crave. Peace with God—a deep and lasting intimacy with our Creator.

However, there is only one way to this peace. Our sole source of serenity comes through the way paved by the sacrifice of Christ.

Though God is the God of all peace, we cannot experience peace with God without Christ. Only through knowing the Prince of Peace can we experience true and lasting rest for our war-torn and weary souls. Not through self-righteous works. Not through good intentions. Not through any man-made effort.

Jesus is the only way to peace with God.

1. Open with a short prayer. Jot down any areas of unrest in your heart and mind today. As you get ready to study His Word today, ask the Holy Spirit to open your eyes to see the way of peace God has provided for you.

To begin our study of peace today, we'll spend some time in the Book of Ephesians. This is taken from a letter written by Paul, about 30 years after the death of Christ, to encourage and guide the Christians in the city of Ephesus. Much of Paul's ministry was spent helping the new church understand all the implications of the perfect life and sacrificial death of Jesus, our Savior. Most of the people of the church Paul was writing to were known as Gentiles, meaning they were not Jewish and, thus, were not part of the Jewish family of God. After the promised Messiah has come—Jesus the Christ—a new avenue to God was opened. This new road was now accessible to all (not only those of Jewish descent) and Paul wrote the Book of Ephesians to help these brand new and untested Gentile believers to better understand their newfound faith.

Paul continually spoke of Christ. He spent his ministry proclaiming the truths of the Cross and all Christ had done for us. Therefore, it's important for us to pay attention to all that is true about us because of the Cross of Christ.

Before
Christ

The Work
of Christ

After
Christ

By Grace through Faith

2. Read Ephesians 2:12–17. During this first read, look for any words that describe your life before Christ. On the left side of the cross on page 41, write out at least five truths you find. Remember to consult the cheat sheet if you're not sure. *Example: I was separated from Christ (v. 12)*

3. Now read Ephesians 2:12–17 again, this time looking for all the ways we have been changed because of Christ. In other words, what has Jesus provided for you? You might consider writing these truths out as a statement of what is true of you. Jot down at least five of these truths to the right of the cross in your diagram. *Example: I've been brought near to God (v. 13)*

We are born hostile toward God. This word *hostile* (also translated as "enmity" and "hatred") used in Ephesians is a derivative of the root word *enemy*. You and I were enemies of God. In fact, if you are not in Christ today, you still stand in hostility, as an enemy of the very One who can bring you peace. Your hostile attitude can only be removed through faith in all Christ has done for you. Right now you are either far from or near to God, alienated from God or a part of the unified family of God, a hostile enemy of God or at peace with your Holy Creator. In Christ alone peace with God is found.

4. To finish our time together today, turn to Romans 5:1 in your Bible. Read this verse, looking again for what we can learn about peace, then fill in any additional details on the cross diagram.

Though enemies, we are made right with God through the justification that comes with our salvation. Justification is right standing before God—it is "just as if" we'd never sinned. Before Christ, we stand as condemned sinners and enemies of a Holy God. Once we accept, by faith, the work of Christ (His perfect life, payment of sin through His death, and power over sin through His Resurrection) on our behalf, we are clothed in Christ's righteousness and brought into the eternal family of God. Through this justification, hostility with God is banished and peace with God is ushered in.

Because Jesus lived a sinless life, it is as though I do, too. Since my Savior died on the Cross, the debt I owed from the sin I commit is paid in full. And when Christ rose from the grave, showing power over sin and death, He was once again at peace with His Father.

By God's great and glorious grace, through our faith and by the work of Christ on the Cross, we are granted peace with God. If you find yourself attempting to achieve peace with God through any other means (good works, right beliefs, behavior modification) and you are uncertain that this powerful transformation of justification has occurred in your life, I encourage you to check out the Good News section in the appendix. Chat through it with your pastor and/or a trusted friend. Don't walk forward without a certainty of your position before God.

{Jesus, thank You for bringing me peace. Through You, I can stand before God, and He is pleased. I praise You for Your obedience to the Father and Your love-filled, merciful sacrifice on the Cross. I do not deserve it, but I am so thankful for it.}

Bonus Study

Read and write out Philippians 2. Continue to note any truths, promises, and commands from this chapter in your journal.

Cheat Sheet

Before Christ

The Work of Christ

After Christ

By Grace through Faith

I WAS . . .

Separated from Christ (v. 12)

Alienated from the common-wealth of Israel (v. 12)

A stranger to the covenants of promise (v. 12)

Without hope (v. 12)

Without God (v. 12)

Far off (vv. 13, 17)

Separated from God by a wall of hostility (v. 14)

NOW . . .

I've been brought near to God (v. 13)

I've been brought near by the blood of Christ (v. 13)

Jesus is my peace (v. 14)

Jesus has made me one with God (v. 14)

Jesus has broken down the dividing wall of hostility (v. 14)

Jesus has caused peace (v. 15)

I have been reconciled to God through the Cross of Christ (v. 16)

The hostility between God and me has been killed (v. 16)

Peace has been preached to me through Christ (v. 17)

ROMANS 5:1

Justified

Peace with God

Why Don't I Experience the Peace-Filled Life?

→ And let the peace of Christ rule in your hearts. —Colossians 3:15 ←

CHOOSING A MAJOR in college was a daunting task. I spent my first quarter at Auburn University burdened with the pressure of choosing my life's path before I even knew what I wanted to be when I grew up. Somewhere along the line, I received advice to choose a major that required classes I looked forward to taking. For me, those were science courses, and I chose a major filled with fun (to me) classes such as hematology, organic chemistry, and parasitology. To this day, the systems of biology, the structures of anatomy, and the standards of chemistry fascinate me.

God has designed each of us and the universe we live in with such intentional, creative purpose. The cells in our bodies, for instance, are fashioned with amazing and functional detail. Our everyday vitality depends on the ability of our cells to selectively drink in what is necessary for life, purposefully deliver what is needed for the function of other cells, and quickly dispose of that which brings death and decay to the systems in our body.

Just as our cells carefully allow what travels in and out of their tiny units, you and I must learn to be better gatekeepers of what we allow to penetrate our hearts and minds.

1. Take some time to express to God whatever lays heavy on your heart today. It is easy to allow discouragement to overwhelm us. He knows. He hears. He loves. Because of all Jesus has done for us in His death and Resurrection, God sees us through the perfect life and sacrifice of His Son. All shame, guilt, and separation is gone. Even if you have a hard time believing it, thank God for the complete forgiveness of your sin, the great grace you've received, and the unconditional love He has for you.

So far in our study of everyday peace, we've established that peace comes only from God. However, sin blocks us from a relationship with the God of all peace. The way to peace with God and the promise of everyday peace was paved for us through the sacrifice of Christ. However, many of us (even though we are in relationship with God) do not experience His peace-filled presence through-out our days. This begs the question: why? Colossians 3:15 gives us insight into one reason why Christians do not experience His peace in our everyday lives.

2. Read Colossians 3:15 and note below what this verse commands us.

2 Peter 1:3–4 tells us that we have been granted "precious and very great" promises from God. It also states we have been granted the "divine power" of His Spirit and, therefore, have all we need to live a life of godliness. God has equipped and empowered me in such a way that I can live out the command to let the peace of Christ rule me. Yet there is often a disconnect with what I know to be true and what my actions show. When this is the case, something other than the peace of Christ dictates the direction of my heart.

The original word used here for *rule* means to be like an umpire, calling the shots. I am to control, rule, and direct every emotion and thought I encounter. Something is always calling the shots and if it is anything but the peace of Christ—which came to me through the gospel—my experience of the very peace I've been promised is sabotaged.

3. When faced with stressful situations or discouraging relationships, who or what tends to be your "umpire"? What typically guides your reactions in those situations?

4. Read John 14:27. Here, Jesus is speaking to His disciples and preparing them, as He begins to make His journey to the Cross. In the space below, write out this verse.

A troubled, fearful heart comes easily, doesn't it? We must fight our sinful, human default response to our everyday difficult moments and allow the peace of God and all He has promised to rule—be the umpire of—our heart's response. When the future is scary and uncertain, or a person you thought was your friend spreads gossip and discord, "let not your hearts be troubled." When an unexpected expense pops up, after an already tight financial season, "neither let [your heart] be afraid." In every potential worry, fear, and failure, we must be selective with what we allow to permeate our hearts. In 2 Corinthians 10:5, Paul encourages us to "take every thought captive." Just as our cells allow life-giving molecules to enter in and actively push disease-causing toxins out, we have a continual regulatory work to do.

5. To close our time together today, read the prayer in 2 Thessalonians 3:16. Write it out below, replacing every instance of "you" to "me." Read it aloud, as a prayer to God.

At all times. In every way. Peace cannot be created. Peace is a gift. God is the grantor. You and I are the recipients and we've already been given peace through Christ. In order to experience this peace in our every moment, we must learn to become better gatekeepers of our thoughts and emotions. Instead of allowing the whims of our hearts and the bondage of our thoughts to rule us, we must draw near to our God and let the realities of His presence guide our hearts and minds.

Let the peace of God rule.

{God, grant me a deeper awareness of the battle for my heart. Help me, Holy Spirit, to guard my heart and allow Your peace to rule through my every moment. Forgive me for the many times I have allowed comparison, fear, selfishness, and comfort to rule my heart instead of Your peace. Thank You for Your grace.}

 *Bonus Study*

Read and write out Philippians 3. Continue to note any truths, promises, and commands from this chapter in your journal.

Cheat Sheet

2. Read Colossians 3:15 and note below what this verse commands us.

- let the peace of Christ rule in my heart
- be thankful

How to Defend Everyday Peace

Put on the whole armor of God, that you may be able to stand against the schemes of the devil. —Ephesians 6:11

SEATED AND CURLED UP on a white, comfy sofa, surrounded by some of my favorite women in the world, a tidal wave of negative emotion swept over me. These women and I met in a cozy cottage for our yearly retreat to process, plan, and pray for our ministries. Hours and hours were spent sharing our hearts, processing our dreams, and preparing to receive God's next steps for our lives. I love these women. It is an absolute treat, honor, and dream to be amongst these beautiful, godly, influential leaders. But what was supposed to be an encouraging, uplifting weekend quickly turned into cause for inner turmoil.

From the moment my plane touched down in Waco, I began to hear the lies: *You're not enough. You don't belong here.* Suddenly, what was once a group full of safety and grace became a space filled with insecurity and fear. Internally, I was spinning out of control. My dear, discerning friend Heather could sense that I was unraveling and cornered me to process what was going on. A floodgate of emotions opened up. Every thought I was able to articulate was filled with lies, insecurities, and unnecessary fear. I knew it. She knew it. But it was freeing to get it all out on the table.

I had failed to be a good umpire of my thoughts (among women where I normally felt safe to be myself) and had allowed lies and half-truths to penetrate my mind and rob my heart of every-day peace. Instead of taking every thought captive and inviting the peace of God to rule my moments, I let feelings of fear, failure, and inferiority call the shots.

A plan to fight the infiltration was desperately needed.

1. As we begin our study today, ask the Spirit of God to bring you a greater awareness of the lies that steal your peace. Declare your need for His strength and power to expel the lies that steal from the peace-filled life you are given through Christ.

Everyday peace is a gift, and I must learn to defend it relentlessly. When I live on guard instead of on vacation, I am better able to recognize the schemes of the evil one who continually attempts to divert me away from intimacy with Jesus. You and I are in the midst of a great battle, and the evil one employs most of his fight-ing tactics on our thought-life. Just as He did in the very first attack on Adam and Eve, he attempts to create doubt in my heart about who God is, and I must be ready to fight off every lie raised against God's character and the goodness of His plan. Today, let's learn how to better defend ourselves. "Be sober-minded; be watchful. Your adversary the devil prowls around like a roaring lion, seeking someone to devour" *(1 Peter 5:8)*.

2. Read Ephesians 6:13–18. In the chart below, note each specific depiction of the armor pieces we've been given, the function of each (if stated), and whether you think it is offensive (used to attack) or defensive (used to protect from attack).

Piece of Armor	Function (if stated)	Offensive or Defensive?
Example: the whole armor of God	to withstand in the evil day; to stand firm	offensive and defensive

This battle for everyday peace is a both defensive and offensive. Truth as a belt protects my most vulnerable places. Because without truth, everything is gray. This is the first line of defense: recognizing an attack. When I know—really know—the truth of who God is, and who I am because of Christ, I can more readily recognize the strikes of deception as they come along.

The breastplate of righteousness guards my heart from despair and accusations, as I stand firm on the promise of all God has done on my behalf. The shoes of peace protect and give me a firm footing on the foundation of the gospel—what the good news of God has done for me through Christ. A shield of faith defends against the onslaught of doubts. The helmet of salvation shields my mind and the thoughts so easily routed away from what is true. Then, finally, the Word of God. My offense and intervention, which brings me back to the first defense of truth, and helps to fill up my arsenal with promises to cling to and truths to fight against the lies, the doubt, the accusations.

3. Read 1 John 2:14. What does John say is true of the "young men"?

4. Read Psalm 119:9–11. What is true in these verses of the "man" who wants to keep from sin? (Let's pretend it's a "woman," as this is just as applicable to us girls, and make our observations as such.)

Abiding, or remaining, in the Word of God (our source of truth) leads to strength to resist the evil one. Instead of being tossed by the whim of my day, emotions, hormones, or circumstances, I can experience the everyday peace of God; and the single most fruitful action I can take toward this everyday peace is to know God's Word. A peaceful state of mind is not something I can create on my own, it is a result of setting my mind on an accurate view of God, continually renewing my mind with the Word and recognizing my need for the Spirit along the way. Because peace is a promised fruit of the Spirit *(Galatians 5:22–23)*—a natural result of the merciful work of God in my life—I only hinder or help the Spirit's work. God is working to bring everyday peace, and I get to come alongside Him and fight for this promised peace.

In the weeks to come, we will look at three specific oppositions to peace: stress, a lack of contentment, and discord in relationships. The bottom line for each is a disconnection from the source of our peace. Though we have peace in our relationship with God (no longer are we His hostile enemies) we still have much to learn about how to walk with the God of peace in our mundane moments. Receiving peace with God doesn't mean we now live in a vacuum with the absence of hardship, stress, and difficult relationships. One day, when we meet Jesus face-to-face in heaven, our daily fears, woes, and worries will be obliterated. Until then, we must learn how to experience the promised peace of God through enjoying the presence of the God who calms every fear, banishes every doubt, and soothes every heartbreak.

{God, give me a heart for Your Word. As stressful situations come my way, bring to mind what is true about who You are, and Your steadfast love for me. Grant me a heart that longs to be in Your presence and the strength to draw near.}

Bonus Study

Read and write out Philippians 4. Continue to note any truths, promises, and commands from this chapter in your journal.

Cheat Sheet

2. Read Ephesians 6:13–18. In the chart below, note each specific depiction of the armor pieces we've been given, the function of each (if stated), and whether you think it is offensive (used to attack) or defensive (used to protect from attack).

Piece of Armor	Function (if stated)	Offensive or Defensive?
the whole armor of God	to withstand in the evil day, to stand firm	offensive and defensive
belt of truth		defensive
breastplate of righteousness		defensive
shoes/gospel of peace	for your feet, readiness	defensive
shield of faith	extinguished all the flaming darts of the evil one	defensive
helmet of salvation		defensive
sword of the Spirit/Word of God		offensive

3. Read 1 John 2:14. What does John say is true of the "young men"?

They are strong.

The Word of God abides in them.

They overcome the evil one.

4. Read Psalm 119:9–11. What is true in these verses of the "man" who wants to keep from sin? (Let's pretend it's a "woman," as this is just as applicable to us girls, and make our observations as such.)

She guards her way according to God's Word.

She seeks Him with all her heart.

She stores up God's Word in her heart to avoid sin.

Summation

→ *Keep your heart with all vigilance, for from it flow the springs of life.* ←
—*Proverbs 4:23*

JUST LAST NIGHT I found myself restless. My body begged for slumber, yet my mind tossed and turned with all my to-do's, my gut churned with anxiety, and my heart longed for the success and influence of others. Under the weather, I had spent much of my day in bed, miserably congested, and mindlessly scrolling through posts on blogs, Instagram, and Facebook. A shift in my heart followed what my mind's eye was engaged in: what I don't have that others possess and what I must do to catch up to them. I even made a mental list of other's imperfections, leading my heart toward a contentious place.

I forfeit peace when I let the influence of others trump the truths of who Christ says I am. Secure. Loved. Protected. Guided. Treasured. Significant. Enough. All through His work on the Cross. When I forget these truths and attempt to live life seeking out the significance, safety, and intimacy I already have in Jesus, peace slips away and its antagonists fill its place.

I must fight for what I know to be true instead of answering to what I feel to be true.

Respond to God's Word

Today, let's take some time to slow down and digest what we've been learning. Remember, this is when we begin to answer the question, "How should what I've learned transform me?"

1. Take a deep breath, and ask the Holy Spirit to fill your heart today as you reflect on all you've learned this week. Ask Him to bring clarity and reveal an action you can take based on at least one specific truth.

2. Circle below the words that best describe what your heart is filled with today.

   worry   joy   anxiety   peace   thankfulness
   calm   criticism   fear   dread   comparison

3. How much of each peace-stealer is present in your everyday moments? Circle the number that best represents your experience of each. *(1=very little present in my life, 10=rules my life)*

   Stress

   1 •••• 2 •••• 3 •••• 4 •••• 5 •••• 6 •••• 7 •••• 8 •••• 9 •••• 10

   Discontentment with my stage and season of life

   1 •••• 2 •••• 3 •••• 4 •••• 5 •••• 6 •••• 7 •••• 8 •••• 9 •••• 10

   Relational Discord

   1 •••• 2 •••• 3 •••• 4 •••• 5 •••• 6 •••• 7 •••• 8 •••• 9 •••• 10

4. Am I attempting to find my peace in something other than God? (ie My circumstances? Control? Another person?)

5. How good am I at guarding my heart and mind against anxiety? Am I being selective in what I allow into my life (like our cells, which we talked about in Day 3) or do I have an open gate for any thought, worry, and attitude to affect my heart and mind?

6. Take another look at the parts of the armor of God you've been given. Which piece of the armor do you most need today? Why?

Everyday peace is not something we can create, it is something that is born in us as we remember Christ and His great love for us, recognize our desperation for the Spirit of God to continue the work He has started in each of us, and renew the patterns of our minds with the powerful, transforming Word of God.

> *{Father, I praise You for all You've done to bring me close to Your heart. Jesus, thank You for making a way for me to have peace with God for eternity. Holy Spirit, I need You. Every moment of every day. I am absolutely unable to successfully guard my heart and renew my mind without Your prompting, Your leading, and Your carrying.}*

Peace in My Everyday Stress

FOCUSING ON
PHILIPPIANS 4:4–9

Foundation

FOCUSing on Philippians 4:4–9

→ *You keep him in perfect peace whose mind is stayed on you, because he trusts* ←
in you. —Isaiah 26:3

I DON'T KNOW much about a soundboard, frequencies, and all the technology involved, but years of singing on various praise teams has allowed me to pick up a few useful tips about sound equipment. A common source of panic for the sound booth is feedback: the high-pitched, loud squall anyone would recognize as bad news. When this occurs, the source of the problem needs to be terminated. Immediately. Typically, it's the case of a microphone picking up sound from the speaker. Since the speaker's job is to amplify sound out to the audience, if a microphone hooked up to the system picks up the sound coming out of the speaker, it begins a never-ending amplification of the sound. A feedback loop. What started as a small (even beautiful) noise is swiftly amplified into an ear-piercing squeal. If left unchecked, the feedback will damage the speakers.

I can easily find myself stuck in a similar feedback loop of anxiety. Stress is inevitable. It cannot be entirely avoided and the presence of it in my life is not inherently bad. What I do with the stress is another story. My response to stress will either promote or cripple my everyday peace.

1. Open your time in Philippians 4:4–9 with a prayer dedicating this week's study to God. Thank Him for His words about anxiety, and ask Him to open your eyes to the truths contained in this week's verses. Ask Him for the grace and strength to obey and follow in His ways.

Enjoy Every Word

2. Today we'll work through our first layer of studying Philippians 4:4–9 by rewriting the passage. Our Foundation work is designed to help us slow down and begin to grasp what is going on in this passage. Below and on the following page, you can write out the verses word-for-word, diagram them, or draw pictures or symbols to help you begin to understand what is being said. There is no right or wrong way to do this. It is simply an exercise of intentionally absorbing each word. We'll build on what we learn from this practice throughout the rest of the week. If you are super-short on time today, read the passage then write out verses 6–7.

3. Which words or phrases in Philippians 4:4–9 impacted you today? Consider writing out these verses on a 3-by-5 card and posting it in your house or office space as a reminder.

4. Write out any questions you have about this passage. Your questions should be answered by the end of the week as you continue to study. If not, you'll have an opportunity to consult Bible commentaries.

A quick glance at today's news, my schedule, maybe even my bank account, causes me to begin experiencing distress. I cannot escape the weights of this world, but I do have a choice in how I respond. Regardless of its source, I experience anxiety when I ignore who God is. When I forget the power, grace, perspective, and love He freely gives, I have no choice but to take the stressors upon myself. This self-dependence leads to anxiety—the negative cycle of overwhelming pressure and utter hopelessness—which proceed to drive and dictate my heart and mind.

This anxiety feedback loop is a result of leaving God out of the stress equation.

Stress demands a response. If left unchecked, it will wreak havoc on our hearts, minds, and everyday lives. Instead of allowing the weight of our world to crush us, let's remember the burden of all our problems is not ours to bear. "Take my yoke upon you, and learn from me, for I am gentle and lowly in heart, and you will find rest for your souls" *(Matthew 11:29)*. This week we'll look at the role we play in finding victory over this anxiety, which steals our everyday peace.

> *{God, I am thankful that I don't have to live a life filled with anxiety! Help me to remember these verses today as I attempt to guard my heart with the promises of Your Word. I have much to rejoice in. You are a God who hears my requests. You, the God of peace, will be with me today!}*

 *Bonus Study*

Choose your favorite translation of Philippians 4:4–9 and write it out on 3-by-5 cards. Keep the verses with you, post them up around your house, and commit them to memory.

Observation

FOCUSing on Philippians 4:4–9

Therefore, my brothers, whom I love and long for, my joy and crown, stand firm thus in the Lord, my beloved. —Philippians 4:1

I GO THROUGH spurts of attending gym classes. It's a joy when my schedule allows for me to make the classes I love. However, there are many times when my calendar conflicts with my morning fitness hour. So I stop going, and I feel it. My energy lowers (and my willpower to make good food choices plummets with it). The silly thing is, I have access to our gym 24/7, but I get stuck in feeling I've missed the boat if I miss my morning class. Later, my schedule shifts and the time slot opens back up; however, by then I feel out of shape, lacking energy, and completely void of motivation to get back into the rhythm of going to the gym. Before long, I dread the classes I missed so much because I don't want my out-of-shape self to be seen. This silliness keeps me in a lethargy loop, hindering me from the very thing I need to replenish the energy, motivation, and health I desire. To step out of this loop, I need truth. I must tell myself what I know to be true about exercise, even when my lazy body is telling me otherwise.

The anxiety loop is no different. To escape anxiety, I must learn to preach truth to myself and allow it to penetrate my heart in such a way that it affects my actions. Paul calls this personal truth-preaching *standing firm (Philippians 1:27; 4:1; Galatians 5:1;*

2 Thessalonians 2:15). Standing firm is a continual staying, a constant clinging, an abiding persevering toward what God's Word tells me is true about Him. My Refuge is safe, secure, and available to me in each struggle I walk through. My Provider is present, powerful, and worthy of praise in all predicaments. My Deliverer is dependable, capable, and devoted to my good in every difficulty I face. And though these attributes are always true, I forfeit the peace that comes from His presence when I forget who He is. There are unfathomable joys and a soul-deep peace that only come from abiding—standing firm—in His presence. "Those who live in the shelter of the Most High will find rest in the shadow of the Almighty" *(Psalm 91:1 NLT).*

1. Open your time with God today by writing out a prayer in the space below, expressing your eagerness to learn more about the peace He offers. Ask the Holy Spirit for His wisdom and revelation as we dive deeper into the truths held in these verses.

Look at the Details

2. As you read Philippians 4:4-9 today, look first for all the commands in these verses and fill in the chart below with what you find. (Check out the cheat sheet at the end of today's study if you get stuck.)

Commands in Philippians 4:4-9

It'd be easy to start a checklist at this point: Pray. Ponder. Practice. Anxiety knocks at the door, and we begin a three-step program to kick her to the curb. Problem is, self-effort only takes us so far, and soon we find ourselves pursuing a state of man-made peace that never lasts. We turn God into a vending machine. Pray to God + ponder "these things" + practice "these things" = dissipated anxiety. However, the antidote to anxiety is not in my actions alone. Peace comes in remembering and resting in who God is and who I am because of Christ.

3. Now read the passage again, this time observe verses 7 and 9, and list out any promises you see.

Promises in Philippians 4:4–9

4. We are promised the peace of God twice in this passage. Look back at Philippians 4:7 and note below what is true about this peace. How does Paul (author of the Book of Philippians) describe this peace?

We must stand firm in God's provision for us, as if our feet are cemented to His grace. Because the promised peace of God is found in God's grace alone. If I set out to end the toxic effects of anxiety in my life by standing firm in anything other than the work of God on my behalf, whatever peace may come will be temporary. From this platform of grace, we then pray, ponder, and practice. We pray because it is oxygen to us—this connection to the God of all peace—because we know He loves to hear from us. We ponder "these things" because they train our mind to remember who God is and who we are because of Christ. Pondering reminds me of the grace in which I stand. We practice "these things" not because we are supposed to but because we want to—out of an overflow of worship to our glorious God.

{*God, give me a glimpse of Your surpassing, unending peace. I long for more of it in my life. I need You, and You alone, to provide peace for my every moment. Set my heart toward "these things"—which are true, honorable, just, pure, lovely, commendable, excellent, and worthy of praise. Holy Spirit, draw my heart to more and more of Your Word so that I may store it in my heart to dwell on throughout the day.*}

Bonus Study

Read Matthew 6:25–34 and write out the commands and promises given in this passage.

Cheat Sheet

2. As you read Philippians 4:4-9 today, look first for all the commands in these verses and fill in the chart below with what you find.

Commands in Philippians 4:4-9

Rejoice (twice) v. 4

Let your reasonableness be known to everyone v. 5

Do not be anxious about anything v. 6

Let your requests be made known to God v. 6 (How? In everything, by prayer and supplication, with thanksgiving)

Think about "these things": whatever is true, honorable, just, pure, lovely, commendable, excellent, worthy of praise v. 8

Practice "these things": what you have learned and received and heard and seen from the leaders around me v. 9

3. Now read the passage again, this time observe verses 7 and 9, and list out any promises you see.

Promises in Philippians 4:4-9

The peace of God will guard my heart and mind (v. 7)

The God of peace will be with me (v. 9)

4. We are promised the peace of God twice in this passage. Look back at Philippians 4:7 and note below what is true about this peace. How does Paul (author of the Book of Philippians) describe this peace?

Surpasses all understanding

Clarification

FOCUSing on Philippians 4:4–9

> ↠ *We do not know what to do, but our eyes are on you.* —*2 Chronicles 20:12* ↞

FROM THE STACKS of work with pressing deadlines to the never-ending piles of laundry that taunt me daily, I often experience help-lessness in the face of pressure to perform and produce. When I begin to feel the overwhelming waves of responsibilities and expec-tations crash all around me, I give in to paralysis. Instead of stand-ing up to the waves, by pushing them back with the truth that my identity is not tied to my performance, I choose to lay there, beaten and bruised by all the what-ifs and the if-onlys. I allow anxiety free reign of my heart.

Over 2,500 years ago, a king faced an obstacle that puts my problematic laundry mounds to shame. This king, Jehoshaphat, received the news of enemy attack, and his people awaited an imminent invasion of a "great multitude" *(2 Chronicles 20:2)*. At the news of this pending raid, the Bible tells us King Jehoshaphat was afraid—but what came after this visceral fear reaction is of note: "Then Jehoshaphat was afraid and set his face to seek the Lord" *(v. 3)*. With much opportunity to be anxious, Jehoshaphat chose rightly and sought his Deliverer—his only hope for victory.

After turning His own heart toward total dependence on the grace of God, Jehoshaphat turned to lead His people.

He addressed them with important charges: do not be afraid or dismayed *(vv. 15, 17)* and stand firm and see the salvation of the Lord on your behalf *(v. 17)*. Accompanying these commands were two promises to cling to: the battle is not yours but God's *(v. 15)* and the Lord will be with you *(v. 17)*. The nation of Judah still needed to line up and face their fierce enemy, but they did so standing on the provision and promise of their faithful and capable Commander. Not Jehoshaphat but their Almighty God.

1. Open today's time with prayer. Thank God for the depths of His living and active Word. Ask Him to make you aware of the places you are not allowing God's Word to penetrate your heart. Ask His Spirit to grant you a willingness to change, especially in the area of anxiety, and the grace to follow in obedience where He leads.

Uncover the Original Meaning

As part of our Clarification day, we come to our Greek study. You may be a bit intimidated by the thought of studying the original language, but it's an important layer we get to peel back. With the right tools, studying the Greek can be as simple as looking up a word in the dictionary. If this is your first attempt at Greek study or you need a refresher, I encourage you to check out the videos I've created to show you how to use many of the online Greek tools. Just head to KatieOrr.me/Resources and look for the VIDEOS section.

DECIDE which word you would like to study.

2. To start your Greek study, look for any potential keywords in Philippians 4:4–9. As you find any repeated word or words that seem important to the passage, write them down below.

Maybe you had the word *anxious* on your list? Let's study this word together.

DISCOVER that word as it was originally written.

Now that you know what you want to study, you need to look up the word *anxious* to find out what the original Greek word is. An Interlinear Bible will show you English verses and line up each word next to the Greek words they were translated from. You can find these tools in print form, but the easiest way to use them is through the many free online websites and/or phone applications I've listed on my website. Many of these resources will make this Discovery step easy to do. You can find the Greek word with a click of a button or tap of the screen.

3. Using your preferred tool, see if you can find the original word for *anxious,* and write it below.

You might have written *merimnaō* or even *μεριμνᾶτε*. The latter is the original Greek word. Most people (including me!) cannot read this, so a phonetic spelling (known as a transliteration) is typically provided. That is where we get *merimnaō*.

For a more detailed explanation of what is going on behind the scenes of your app or website tool, check out How to Do a Greek Word Study in the appendix.

DEFINE that word.

Now that you know the original word for *be anxious* used in Philippians is *merimnaō*, we can look up that Greek word to better define and uncover the original meaning. For this, we will fill out the following chart.

Greek Word:
MERIMNAŌ

Verse and Version:
PHILIPPIANS 4:6 ESV

Part of Speech:	Translation Notes:
(verb, noun, etc.)	(How else is it translated? How often is this word used?)
verb	*take thought (11x), care (5x), be careful (2x), have care (1x)*
Strong's Concordance Number:	Definition:
#3309	*anxious, troubled with cares*
Notes:	
	"to be troubled with cares"

4. Now, why don't you try it on your own? Use the above steps to look up the word *guard* in verse 7 and fill in the chart provided on the following page. (If you are brand new to Bible study this may be overwhelming to you. That's OK. It was for me, as well. Instead, consider looking up a few words in the dictionary and write out their definitions. This is still a great way to do our Clarification work of better understanding the meaning of each word.)

Greek word: *Verse and Version:*

_____   _____

Part of Speech: *(verb, noun, etc.)*	Translation Notes: *(How else is it translated? How often is this word used?)*
Strong's Concordance Number:	Definition:
Notes:	

5. What discoveries did you make through your Clarification study?

I love the story of Jehoshaphat. This example of trust in God as our only hope brings me much comfort, hope, and practical steps to take when I find myself stymied by anxiety. Only God can bring victory over that which causes me anxiety. And as I stand firm in all of who God is—present, capable, powerful—I can face whatever comes my way. Not because I am strong, but because my Savior is. The battle for whatever causes me anxiety belongs to the Lord. I am but a simple soldier striving to remain with my capable Commander who alone can prevent the hostile invasion of my heart. He is my guard and the keeper of my heart and every promise given to me in His Word. I certainly have action to take in this fight for peace, but it is only to remain and stand firm in the provision of my God who is might to save. "The Lord your God is in your midst, a mighty one who will save" *(Zephaniah 3:17)*.

> *{God, I allow too many anxious thoughts to invade my heart. Help me to better understand how You guard my heart to "prevent hostile invasion." Holy Spirit, grant me a deeper awareness of where my thoughts tend to slide. Help me take these thoughts captive and replace them with the truth in Your Word. Thank You in advance for the work you are going to do in my heart and mind!}*

Bonus Study

Follow the Greek study steps for as many words in Philippians 4:4–9 as time allows. Feel free to simply look up the definition for the Greek word, especially if this is your first try. There is much to be learned even in that!

Cheat Sheet

Greek word:

PHROUREO

Verse and Version:

PHILIPPIANS 4:7 ESV

Part of Speech:	Translation Notes:
(verb, noun, etc.)	(How else is it translated? How often is this word used?)
verb	_guard (3), captive (1)_

Strong's Concordance Number:	Definition:
_#5432_	_guard; watch_

Notes:

"to guard, protect by a military guard, either to prevent hostile invasion . . . to protect by guarding, to keep."

Utilization

FOCUSing on Philippians 4:4–9

» *In God I trust; I shall not be afraid.* —Psalm 56:4 «

MY YOUNGEST CHILD is a wild canon. Full of energy, everything is a game to my sweet Michael. Several times recently, he has run toward me, ready to jump into my arms. Problem was, my attention was elsewhere. Thankfully, at the last moment I noticed a flash of boy darting my way, and I was able to hold my arms out just in time to save him from falling flat on the floor. I'm thankful my sweet son views me as safe and inviting enough to blindly trust that Mommy will always catch him. Though I am an imperfect and sometimes inattentive mother, he runs to me still.

I long to have the same view of my Father God that Michael has for me. Oftentimes I slip into the opposite view of my own heavenly parent. Instead of holding to the biblical portrait of who God is, I allow my limited mind's eye to dictate my belief of who God is. How I view God affects everything about me. If my view of God is small, weak, and disinterested, I will not run to Him with the same abandon, excitement, and trust as my energetic five year old. Instead, I wallow in fearful thoughts and fret about the future. I remain frozen by anxiety when I could be resting safely in the arms of my capable, attentive Father.

1. Take some time to evaluate your anxiety levels this week. As particular anxious thoughts come to mind write them down, acknowledge them to God, then bring a specific request to Him in regards to that situation. Find something within that situation to thank God for.

Discover the Connections

2. Read Philippians 4:4-9 to start your study today.

3. For our Utilization study, we'll simply look up verses related to any word or phrase we want to learn more about. Today, let's start with the phrase, "do not be anxious about anything," in verse 6. Look up each following reference and take note of any truths that reveal a bigger picture of the threads this verse is attached to. You might consider applying one or more of the FOCUS method steps to that passage, depending on the time you have for the day. I typically enjoy listing out truths I see, especially those that help me understand the original passage I'm studying. You can write out the passage in the space provided, or even look up a Greek word or two in your interlinear Bible. Just do what interests you and what you have time for!

Philippians 4:6—"do not be anxious about anything"

1 Peter 5:6–7

Matthew 6:25–34

Psalm 55:22

God clothes the grass of the field with beauty and crafts the splendor of the lilies. He brings provisions for the birds of the air to flourish and spend their day in flight. He is a God of details, beauty, and abundance. Yet if I see Him as stingy, careless, and distant, I'll not naturally turn to Him in my need.

4. To close out our study today, look up Psalm 56:8 and note the actions God takes toward us.

God keeps my tears in a bottle. He counts my every tossing. He also knows every hair on my head *(Matthew 10:30)* and every move I make *(Psalm 139:2)*. He is lovingly near, not apathetically distant. He is intimately acquainted, not carelessly detached. He is powerfully proficient, not totally incapable. I must fight for this view of God. Because, though it is who the God of the Bible is, it is not always the God I depict in my mind's eye. So when I notice my view of God has become small, I awaken myself to the truth that my God is able. More than able. When stress throws me a curveball of fearful thoughts, I pass it right on to Jesus. When worry leaves a heavy weight on my heart, I tear it off like a jacket and lay it upon my God's capable shoulders. When anxiety crushes me into a corner, I do the only thing I can do: cry out for rescue from my caring, capable God.

My only hope.

> *{God, the battle against anxiety is overwhelming. Help me to cast my cares onto You, instead of holding on to them myself. Remind me again and again how much You love me. You know and care about every detail of my life. Thank You for being a personal, present, caring God.}*

Bonus Study

Look up cross-references for additional phrases in this week's passage that you would like to learn more about. Continue until you need to move on with your day. If your Bible does not have cross-references in it, check out the online cross-referencing recommendations at KatieOrr.me/Resources. You could easily spend two or three days, 15 minutes or more at a time, working through each verse. Remember, these days are simply suggestions. Follow God's leading. If He tells you to slow down and dig deep, go for it!

Summation

FOCUSing on Philippians 4:4–9

» *Behold, I am the Lord, the God of all flesh. Is anything too hard for me?* «
—Jeremiah 32:27

HE CAN'T. HE WON'T. So, I must.

This is what I am declaring when I attempt to fight anxiety without God. I am saying that God is weak and disinterested and cannot—or will not—take care of me. Instead of bringing my every tear and trouble to the presence of God, I mull over situations, attempt to manage stress, and medicate symptoms*. But the battle for peace is not won by merely removing that which triggers our anxious response. While there may certainly be wise adjustments that can be made to alleviate sources of stress in my life, anxiety cannot simply be managed. It must be eradicated. The presence of God's peace in my life is the opposite of anxiety. As long as I live on this sin-scorched earth, I will encounter continual and legitimate causes for moments, even seasons of stress. The fight for peace is won as I remember—regardless of what I feel and what I can or cannot see—the victory is already won and my Commander is powerful, mighty to save.

*I know there are certain physical conditions in which medication is needed to alleviate anxiety. I have been on medication for depression for a time, as a means to an end goal of a healthier thought life and needed energy from a (then undiagnosed) thyroid condition. Please know I do not condemn the use of medication to help us move toward a better practice of God's peace, and I'm so thankful for the blessing of modern medicine. I pray the Lord will give you wisdom as you navigate treatment options.

Respond to God's Word

Today, let's take some time to slow down and digest what we've been learning by going through our Summation steps. Remember, this is when we begin to answer the question, "How should what I've learned affect me?" To do this we will do three things:

1. **Identify**—Find the main idea of the passage.

2. **Modify**—Evaluate my beliefs in light of the main idea.

3. **Glorify**—Align my life to reflect the truth of God's Word.

Ask God to stir your heart toward application (if He hasn't already!). Spend a few moments committing to walk ahead in obedience to all God has shown you this week.

IDENTIFY—Find the main idea of the passage.

1. Take a few moments to flip back to each day's study to review what you've learned this week.

2. In the space below, write out Philippians 4:4–9 in your own words. Or simply write out what you think the main idea of this passage is in regard to our study of peace.

3. Read a commentary or study Bible to see how your observations from this week line up with the scholars. (You can find links to free commentary options as well as in-print investment suggestions at KatieOrr.me/Resources.) As you search commentaries, ask God to make clear the meaning of any passages that are fuzzy to you. Record any additional observations below.

MODIFY—Evaluate my beliefs in light of the main idea.

Prayerfully journal through the following questions, asking for the Spirit of God to enlighten and convict you.

4. Are you fighting for everyday peace by pursuing the presence of God, or are you expecting peace to come automatically to each moment?

5. Do you typically dwell more on "these things" (true, pure, etc.) or the cares of your everyday moments? Why?

6. Do you tend to cast your cares on God or hold on to them? Why?

GLORIFY—Align my life to reflect the truth of God's Word.

7. What might it look like to allow the peace of Christ to rule in your anxious places today?

8. What actions can you take to better renew your mind with the truth of who God is?

9. Pick one action, and write it down below. Ask God for the grace to walk obediently this week as you battle anxiety with truth.

When I take God out of the stress equation and hold on to the cares of my life, I attempt to live life on my own. I say, *I don't need God—I can do this on my own.* That very declaration ignores the salvation and grace afforded to me at the Cross. Jesus died to bring me into forever fellowship with God. It was not solely to reconcile me for the moment of salvation. He sacrificed Himself to bring me abundant life. Today. Tomorrow. Forever. The Cross of Christ is so much more than the way to heaven. The Cross is also the way to a life full of peace through the constant, caring, and powerful presence of God.

> *{I need You, God. I have no hope for change without Your grace. Be my strength. Open my eyes. Change my heart. Be glorified in me!}*

Peace in Any Circumstance

FOCUSING ON
PHILIPPIANS 4:10–13

Foundation

FOCUSing on Philippians 4:10–13

→ But godliness with contentment is great gain. —1 Timothy 6:6 ←

OUR TRIP TO China brought about many opportunities for change and growth. I look back on that trip with much joy and wonderment. I want to go back. The people are generous and gentle and the food (which is nothing like American "Chinese" food) is fantastic. My husband Chris and I had a seven month old at the time, and I was a mom on the go. After I had my first child, I pressed on into my work and ministry and simply brought him along for the ride. It was a fun and fulfilling season of life.

And then, China. The first few days of our trip were a nightmare, beginning with our first hour in the country. After 20 hours of travel under our belt, and exhaustion more than setting in, we had one leg of our excursion remaining. We'd successfully navigated the boarding of our final flight from Beijing only to sit in the very hot, stuffy, cigarette smoke-filled body of a parked plane. We had no idea why we were parked, and how long it would be until takeoff. We couldn't understand a word of the flight attendant's announcements, and the one girl on our team who could understand the language was aisles and aisles away. After an all-too-spicy, not-sure-what-this-is onboard meal, another hour of smoke inhalation, and several more announcements spoken only in Mandarin Chinese, we finally made it into the air.

Finally, we arrived at our destination to quickly find ourselves in an environment that was not at all stroller-friendly. Over the days to come, I learned that elevators and escalators were sparse, and the few available were almost always nonfunctional. Also, this part of the world is not the cleanest of spaces by my Western standards. I don't consider myself a big germ freak, but growing up in America, with our restaurant health ratings posted on the wall and our abundant hand sanitizer dispensers, I was thrown a bit aback at the disparities. And the seven month old? He was more than over being a world traveler.

My contented, peaceful season of life was hastily and completely interrupted. I was consumed with everything that was going wrong and how hard life had become. Sometimes, new chapters of life come in like a storm. Other times, they slide in slow as a snail. Regardless of how difficulties come, they often reveal that my heart is not truly at peace. Because a satisfaction with life that is dependent on electronic stairs for my stroller and things going just as planned is not contentment at all.

1. To begin this week's study, write out a prayer asking God to allow you to see the state of your heart. Consider following the pattern of this prayer from Psalm 139:23-24: "Search me, O God, and know my heart! Try me and know my thoughts! And see if there be any grievous way in me, and lead me in the way everlasting!"

2. Circle the place that best describe your contentment over the past few months. *(1=struggling to enjoy my life, 10=peace-filled moments, regardless of my circumstances)*

1 •••• 2 •••• 3 •••• 4 •••• 5 •••• 6 •••• 7 •••• 8 •••• 9 •••• 10

3. Write down any words that come to mind regarding this level of contentment.

Enjoy Every Word

4. Today we'll work through our first layer of studying Philippians 4:10-13 by rewriting the passage. Remember, our Foundation work is designed to help us slow down while we read the passage. Do what best helps you enjoy each word.

5. Which words or phrases in Philippians 4:10–13 impacted you today? Consider writing out these verses on a 3-by-5 card and hanging it around the house or your office space as a reminder.

6. Write out any questions you have about this passage. Your questions should be answered by the end of the week as you continue to study. If not, you'll have an opportunity to consult commentaries.

According to dictionary.com, contentment is to be "satisfied with what one is or has; not wanting more or anything else." Contentment is hard to come by. It is not a guest that arrives naturally or stays willingly. Contentment is an enduring peace that is independent of circumstance.

Dependent peace is no peace at all.

{God, I confess my tendency to desire that which I don't have. I also disregard and wish away certain aspects of the blessings You have given me. Lead me toward a settled confidence in the season and circumstances You have allowed in my life. Help me to always remember that You are a good God. Help me to treasure the good gifts You give me, and keep my eye from wandering toward what others have.}

Bonus Study

Look up the following verses, noting what is true about mankind.

Job 1:21

Ecclesiastes 5:15

1 Timothy 6:7

Write out a summary statement of these observations.

How do you think this perspective (or lack thereof) shapes your contentment?

Observation

FOCUSing on Philippians 4:10 – 13

We are treated . . . as having nothing, yet possessing everything.
— *2 Corinthians 6:8, 10*

AFTER THOSE FIRST few days of Asian trial-by-fire, my lack of contentment with the inconveniences of a foreign country were quickly realized, and within a few days (by God's gracious and gentle hand of correction) my heart turned toward gratefulness and amazement of my new surroundings. Five years after my summer in China, I found my soul in a much different place and another new country. A fraction of the distance away, I spent eight days on missions in the Mapou village of La Gonave, an island tucked inside the west coast of mainland Haiti. The lack of every kind of advance in this country is astounding, especially with it being in America's backyard. Traveling to La Gonave is a time-warp journey.

Nestled in red clay mountains, most of the "road" to Mapou is so tumultuous that it takes two very bumpy hours in a truck to drive a mere 15 miles. In this mountainous, rocky village, all the food available is grown through rock-filled crops, harvested from native fruit trees, or acquired through trade at the local *marché*. The coastal villagers bring fish, conch, and other finds from the sea, while the inlanders bring corn, watermelon, plantains, or whatever is in season at the time. When the winter months come, and the crops are gone, there is very little to eat. Many may go long periods of time without food.

There is no electricity, running water, or lakes, springs, or wells. They are wholly dependent on rain for survival. On the International Ministry of Hope "compound" where we stayed, we had a few hours of generated power in the evening so we could eat dinner and prepare for bed. Bathrooms stalls had been built for mission teams, like us, where we could take bucket "showers" with water from the cistern. Any leftover liquid was then poured into the tank of one of few porcelain toilets on the island. This was so we had something to flush through the bowl later on when needed. Our meals were pre-pared by hired hands in an itty-bitty hut over charcoal made from trees in the area.

Though almost every modern convenience is absent, the vil-lage is filled with friendly, giving people. Children laugh joyfully and play with abandon as they enjoy the soccer balls we brought them. Most attended the weeklong Vacation Bible School we hosted wearing the only clothes they owned—some without a pair of shoes to their name. As we ministered to the children, we observed the men and women of the village working heartily and gratefully to provide what little they could for their family.

Watching these beautiful people made me wonder the secret of their contentment. My soul flew to Haiti excited to serve, but also thankful for the respite from the throes of three little ones ages five and under—altogether dependent on me for their eating, dress-ing, sleeping, and waking. (Actually, I take that back—they had no problem waking. Way too early, in fact.)

I felt cornered and crushed by my stage of life. Limited. Lonely. Lacking fulfillment in my everyday living. The promise of everyday peace felt like a sham. But these men and women—who had so little—possessed a peaceful countenance independent of circumstances.

1. Ask the Holy Spirit to continue His gentle work on your heart, as you move toward a place of contentment in every circumstance.

Look at the Details

2. Read Philippians 4:10–13 again, and fill in the chart below with the truths of Paul's experience. (Check out the cheat sheet at the end of today's study if you get stuck.)

What Paul Learned	What Paul Knows	What Paul Can Do
"I have learned . . ."	*"I know how to . . ."*	*"I can do . . ."*

3. Which of these truths stands out to you? Why?

4. To complete our study today, look up 1 Timothy 6:6–8. Read it and note below what you learn about contentment.

Though the people of Haiti lack the many modern conveniences I have, they also lack the vast and varied voices that declare what I should have, must do, and what is supposed bring me happiness. Because contentment (and discontentment) is learned. Too often I listen to the wrong teachers: the standards of social media, the opinions of others, the cravings of commercialism. The instruction of these tutors leads only to discontentedness.

The people of Mapou, like Paul, had learned the secret of contentment. Not only did these villagers have very few voices teaching them what they "needed," but many of them had met Jesus and were overcome with a longing to be in His presence. Many walked hours to hear the Word of God preached. They listened intently and eagerly, then stayed behind to ask question after question about their God and His Word until it was finally too dark to read the words in our Bibles. They wanted to learn more and more and more about God. Though they could load up all their possessions in a wheelbarrow, and they did not always know where their next meal would come from, they were rich in spirit and content in Christ.

Most of us can fill a wheelbarrow with the Bibles we have collecting dust around our house, yet we lack this same drive and desperate longing for Jesus to fill our every moment, be our only teacher. "Learn from me, for I am gentle and lowly in heart, and you will find rest for your souls. For my yoke is easy, and my burden is light" *(Matthew 11:29–30)*.

Everyday peace is stolen when I listen to the wrong voice.

{Holy Spirit, speak loudly to me. Help me to identify the voices of others I am listening to, and learn to intentionally turn those teachers away. Point my heart toward Your instruction alone. Grant me a deep desire to learn from You, be with You, and be thankful to You for whatever comes my way today.}

 *Bonus Study*

Read 2 Corinthians 6:3–10 to learn a bit more of the situations Paul found himself in, which led to his contentment. List out all that these "servants of God" endured.

Cheat Sheet

2. Read Philippians 4:10–13 again, and fill in the chart below with the truths of Paul's experience.

What Paul Learned	What Paul Knows	What Paul Can Do
"I have learned . . ."	"I know how to . . ."	"I can do . . ."
• To be content whatever the situation (v. 11) • The secret of facing plenty, hunger, abundance, and need (v.12)	• Be brought low (v. 12) • Abound (v. 12)	• All things through Christ who gives me strength (v. 13)

Clarification

FOCUSing on Philippians 4:10-13

Not that I am speaking of being in need, for I have learned in whatever situation I am to be content. —Philippians 4:11

WHEN I WAS single, I wanted to be married. Once married, I wanted children. While I was in the newborn stage of motherhood, I longed for sleep. Lots and lots of sleep. While pregnant with my third child, we lived in a 1,000-square-foot apartment and longed for more space. Once in a bigger place (and to this day), I missed the ease of keeping such a tiny place tidy. Years and years of smothering Florida summers begged for a break from the constant sweat. Whereas, enduring these frigid Kentucky winters makes me take back any complaint of excess heat.

There is an innate urge within each of us that begs for something more and different than what we currently have. The grass-is-greener mentality has plagued us all. Whether it is our location, relationships, job status, body type, or belongings, we are naturally bent on pining for all we do not have. Thankfully, we are given the Spirit of God within us, who is living, moving, and always working to make us more and more content in Jesus. In this week's passage, Paul calls contentment a secret he has learned. To experience everyday peace, we must also discover this mystery he's uncovered. And when we do, an unsurpassable peace will permeate our every thought, circumstance, and relationship.

1. Pray for insight as you continue to study this week's passage. Confess the areas in which you are struggling to be thankful. Ask Him to reveal to you the secret of being content.

Uncover the Original Meaning

Here we go again! I know that this day can seem daunting and difficult, especially if this is a new skill for you. Just as learning to ride a bike or figuring out the latest technology can be frustrating at times, the rewards of pressing in and continuing on are worth it!

If the thought of studying the Greek is still too much today, consider selecting a few words to look up in the dictionary, then rewrite the verse with the definition in place of the word you looked up. Do what works for you.

DECIDE which word you would like to study.

2. Look for any potential keywords in Philippians 4:10–13. As you find any repeated word or words that seem important to the passage, write them down below.

DISCOVER that word as it was originally written.

3. There are many great words to look up, but I want to make sure you look up at least one today: *content.* Using an interlinear Bible, find the original word for content used in verse 11 and write it below.

CONTENT =

DEFINE that word.

4. Now we can look up the Greek word for *content* and fill out our chart below. I've filled out some of it for you. See if you can fill in the rest.

Greek Word:
AUTARKĒS

Verse and Version:
PHILIPPIANS 4:11 ESV

Part of Speech: (verb, noun, etc.)	Translation Notes: (How else is it translated? How often is this word used?)
Strong's Concordance Number: #842	Definition: anxious, troubled with cares
Notes: "independent of external circumstances"; "manage whatever one has"	

5. Follow the Greek study steps to look up at least one more word in this week's passage. Here are a couple you might choose from:

LEARNED (v. 11, 12)

STRENGTHENS (v. 13)

Greek word: Verse and Version:

_____   _____

Part of Speech:	Translation Notes:
(verb, noun, etc.)	(How else is it translated? How often is this word used?)
Strong's Concordance Number:	Definition:
Notes:	

6. What discoveries did you make through your Clarification study? Which word did you learn the most about? (Remember, if you are still not ready to try studying the Greek, feel free to skip all this. Instead, look up the word in the dictionary and write out the definition. Just do something to help you go deeper into the passage we're becoming more and more familiar with.)

Paul learned the secret of contentment—peace in any circumstance—because Jesus influenced his heart more than his assets, surroundings, or authorities on a given subject. This journey began even before he came to Christ. He attempted to find fulfillment in his achievements, status, and fervor in following all the do's and don'ts. Those unfulfilling pursuits ultimately led him to Jesus, because none of those other things could satisfy. After meeting Christ and entering into an intimate relationship, he continued to experience a wide variety of "plenty and hunger, abundance and need" (v. 12). And, in case we're still not getting it, he states it again and again: Whatever situation. Any situation. Every situation. Contentment can be found.

A key to finding contentment is recognizing that there is emptiness in every situation. Whether my salary is in the six digits or I'm on food stamps, contentment will not come. If I can manage to get back into size six pants or I give way to food's pleasure all the way up to a 26, contentment will not come. I can chase my dreams or have them all realized. Contentment will not come. Whether I finally find a way to keep my house clean or I ignore obligations and drown in laundry, contentment will not come. Everyday peace does not come with a certain set of circumstances; it comes when I realize nothing will fulfill the longing in my heart for more.

Contentment is found in Jesus alone.

{God, I need You. I confess that I don't like "being in need." Help me to learn the secret of facing whatever comes my way (or doesn't come my way) with an unshakable contentment in Your good plan for my life. Give me a glimpse of what it looks like to find my contentment in Your presence.}

Bonus Study

Follow the Greek study steps to look up additional Greek words from our passage.

Cheat Sheet

LEARNED (v. 11) = MANTHANŌ

Greek word:
MANTHANŌ

Verse and Version:
PHILIPPIANS 4:7 ESV

Part of Speech:	Translation Notes:
(verb, noun, etc.)	(How else is it translated? How often is this word used?)
verb	learn (22), studied (1), taught (1), ask(1)
Strong's Concordance Number: #G3129	Definition: to learn, comprehend
Notes:	

"has the basic meaning 'to direct one's mind to something.'"

This is a fun case where two different Greek words were translated into the same English word. Looking up the original usage gives us a fuller meaning of both.

LEARNED (v. 12) = MUEO

Greek word:

___MUEO___

Verse and Version:

___PHILIPPIANS 4:12 ESV___

Part of Speech:	Translation Notes:
(verb, noun, etc.)	(How else is it translated? How often is this word used?)
verb	*only usage of exact wording in New Testament*

Strong's Concordance Number:	Definition:
#G3453	*initiate*

Notes:

"learn a secret; to initiate into the mysteries, hence to instruct;—learned the secret"

Utilization

FOCUSing on Philippians 4:10–13

→ *May the Lord give strength to his people! May the Lord bless his people with peace! —Psalm 29:11* ←

PAUL'S JOURNEY IS incredible. As a member of the Pharisees (an elite and very strict sect of the Jewish culture he grew up in), Paul—then known as Saul of Tarsus—pursued his goals with zeal and excellence. With determination and passion, he sought to prove his commitment to the Hebrew Law by following it with all his might. This included imprisoning, even stoning to death, those who no longer identified with the Law, but followed "The Way" of the crucified Jesus. This passionate yet misguided pursuit brought him down a path of "threats and murder against the disciples of the Lord" (Acts 9:1). God intervened, confronted Saul with the worthlessness of His pursuits, and radically changed his heart and life. With a new God-given name and the same fervor and conviction with which he once pursued the death of Christians, Paul, once the persecutor, became the persecuted. Paul spent the rest of his days bringing the message of eternal life through Christ and much of his life was a series unpleasant trials, unfair pain, and tormenting oppression.

1. Spend some time today in praise of all God has given you. From the shoes on your feet, to the food in your belly, thank Him for as many provisions as you can think of.

Discover the Connections

2. Read Philippians 4:10–13 to start your study today.

3. Look up each cross-reference below and take notes from any passages that reveal a bigger picture of the threads attached to the verse. Record what you learn below.

to be content (v. 11)

Hebrews 13:5

facing plenty and hunger (v. 12)

2 Corinthians 11:23–30 (This is Paul's account of just a glimpse of what he had been through.)

him who strengthens me (v. 13)

2 Corinthians 12:10

4. To wrap up your time today, slowly read Philippians 3:7–9.

Sit for a moment and let the significance of Paul's perspective on the worth of Christ soak in. His view of Jesus is key to knowing the secret to contentment. The secret is this: nothing on this earth will ever satisfy me like being with Jesus. Not a different stage of life, a bigger salary, fewer responsibilities, or losing my love handles. Until I treasure Christ as my only true need, my only worthy pursuit, my only fulfilling hope, my soul will remain unsettled. Until I see every disappointment, disease, and difficulty I face as yet another chance to prove the worth of Christ, I will be disgruntled. Paul learned this secret. It wasn't that he was naturally a thankful person or was born with a contented personality. Paul learned contentment through the emptiness of his varied circumstances—both the easy and the difficult. He knew deep down that unwavering peace comes only in the presence of the One who will never leave him or forsake him.

I can take Paul's word for it, or I can try to find satisfaction in something or someone else. But if I slow down enough to be honest with myself, I've lived enough life to think that maybe Paul was on to something. No person or pleasure, no status or luxury, no amount of money or accomplishments can fill the void in my heart meant to be filled by the presence of God. The quicker I can redirect my long-ings and efforts from temporary to eternal, the quicker I will learn the secret to contentment. Only through inviting God to fill my every longing, and allowing Him to consume my every moment, will my heart be filled with an everyday contentment independent of cir-cumstances.

> *{God, bring me perspective in the difficult places in my life. Grant me a spirit that overflows with thankfulness, especially in the situa-tions where it is hard to praise You. Show me a glimpse of the plan You have for me through these trials.}*

 *Bonus Study*

Look up any additional cross-references in Philippians 4:10–13 that you would like to learn more about. Remember, if your Bible does not have cross-references in it, there are many free and easy-to-use online cross-referencing recommendations at KatieOrr.me /Resources.

Summation

FOCUSing on Philippians 4:10–13

Be content with what you have, for he has said, "I will never leave you nor forsake you."—Hebrews 13:5

WRITING ABOUT PEACE has been quite a journey. My good friend Lara says we have to live the message before we can give the message and she's right. I'm not saying the journey is always fun, but it's rewarding. And I'm so thankful to our gracious Lord for allowing me to be a conduit for His words, His message. First to me. Then to whomever will listen. I pray you will hear the message from this week:

- » **Contentment is** *independent of my circumstances.*

- » **Contentment is** *impeded when I listen to the wrong teacher.*

- » **Contentment is** *issued when I see the emptiness of my circumstances.*

- » **Contentment is** *inviting God to fill my every longing with His love.*

- » **Contentment is** *implemented through the strength of Christ alone.*

The journey to everyday peace is not a one-way flight to contentment land. It is a moment-by-moment fight on the battleground for our heart's affections. This is why Paul declares, "I can do all things through him who strengthens me." When he refers to "all things" he doesn't mean that we can run a marathon or a meet a big deadline. He's referring to all the varied situations he's been in. From honored accolades to house arrests. From comfort and riches to sickness and rags. Paul lived a varied and tumultuous life, but through it all he possessed an unshakable everyday peace through the provision of Christ.

Respond to God's Word

IDENTIFY—Find the main idea of the passage.

1. Take a few moments to flip back to each day's study to review what you've learned this week.

2. In the space below, write out Philippians 4:10–13 in your own words. Or simply write out what you think the main idea of this passage is, especially in regards to our study of peace.

3. Read a commentary or study Bible to see how your observations from this week line up with the scholars. As you search the commentaries, ask God to make clear the meaning of any passages that are fuzzy to you. Record any additional observations below.

MODIFY—Evaluate my beliefs in light of the main idea.

Prayerfully journal through the following questions, asking for the Spirit of God to enlighten and convict you.

4. How does your understanding of the ever-popular and often quoted verse, "I can do all things through him who strengthens me," line up with the context and meaning of these verses?

5. What is one area or situation in which you are currently experiencing discontentment? How could the command we studied last week in Philippians 4:8 (think about "these things") help you learn the secret of contentment in this situation?

6. How are you doing at being the gatekeeper of your everyday thoughts? How does your success or absence of guarding your thoughts affect your contentment levels?

GLORIFY—Align my life to reflect the truth of God's Word.

7. What might the peace of Christ ruling in the discontented places of your heart look like?

8. What adjustments can you make this week to move toward contentment?

9. Pick one adjustment and write it down below. Ask God to help you learn the secret of contentment.

Contentment invites the God of all peace to dwell in every crevice of my life. Contentment allows me to rest in God as my everything. Contentment leads me to view every moment—good or bad—as an opportunity to draw near to God in faith that He is in control, always has a purpose, and is ever worthy of my praise.

> *{Help me, Lord! I am so easily drawn toward imagining how life could be so much better instead of being thankful for what I have. I desperately need you to steer my heart toward learning contentment. By your grace, I will walk forward in thankfulness and contentment.}*

Peace in Dissension

FOCUSING ON
PHILIPPIANS 4:1–3

Foundation

FOCUSing on Philippians 4:1–3

But the meek shall inherit the land and delight themselves in abundant peace. —Psalm 37:11

CONFLICT HAPPENS. IT'S unavoidable. Whether it's an annoying co-worker, community acquaintance who rubs you the wrong way, or a disagreement within your family or circle of friends, drama loves to lurk in the shadows. Eager to make an appearance in moments of frustration, relational rifts are a common thief of everyday peace.

You and I have a choice in how we treat difficult people—the mean ones, the annoying ones, and the ones that seem to derive pleasure from watching us squirm. Yet, when difficulty enters the scene, we usually see one of several typical responses. Some of us flee; conflict enters the room and we run to avoid it at all costs. Others (like myself) take a more direct approach and run at conflict head-on, ready to enter battle. We're fighters. Though these strategies seem to be opposite ends of the spectrum, both responses are rooted in forgetfulness.

Whether I tend to come in fighting or I decide to flee the scene, both actions forget that all people are made in God's image. Every person in my life. Even *that* person. The very one who has hurt me the most is a part of God's creation—extravagantly loved by Him. Every moment I have, even with the most difficult person in my life, is an opportunity to follow the example of Christ and show love. Every ounce of conflict in my life can be used to fuel peace or promote dissension in my days. When I forget who I am without Christ—hopelessly selfish, disobedient, and unloving—I lose perspective on the role I get to play in His purposes here on earth. It's easy to miss the opportunities wrapped up in those frustrating relational fires—the chance to point others to the love and forgiveness of Jesus.

When a relationship rubs me raw, I must remember that this person (though sinful and annoying and maybe even intentionally divisive) is a beloved creation of God and might just be in my life on purpose. (For additional studies on how to love others well, check out my FOCUSed15 Bible study *Everyday Love* at focused15.com.)

1. Spend a few moments praying over the relationships in your life. As individuals come to mind, jot down their names and ask God to give you an overwhelming love and compassion for them. Ask God for the perspective to see them as He sees them and the grace to show them the love of Christ.

WEEK 4
DAY 1

Enjoy Every Word

2. Do your foundation work for Philippians 4:1–3 by reading and writing the passage in whichever way you enjoy most. Have fun with this day!

3. Which words or phrases in Philippians 4:1–3 stand out to you today?

4. Write out any questions you have about this passage. Your questions should be answered by the end of the week, as you continue to study. If not, you'll have an opportunity to consult commentaries.

Relational rifts can easily consume my every moment. But, as upsetting as these times can be, I always have a choice in how I respond to conflict. Whether I want to take flight or stay and fight, I can strive to remember even the most basic truths about myself and the very person with whom I am having trouble. And, may I never forget that God can redeem all things for His glory. As we'll see this week, one of the commands in our passage is to stand firm. When conflict arises I have a choice to stand firm, to continue in the way of peace and let the peace of Christ rule my heart, or to forget the way of God and embrace the road toward relational chaos.

> *{God, help me see the difficult people in my life through Your eyes. Where there is fear, pain, and confusion, bring Your healing and peace. Stir my heart toward reconciliation and unity. Holy Spirit, convict me of the places where I hold onto my stubborn sin instead of being set on loving others, regardless.}*

 *Bonus Study*

Look up and write out 1 Corinthians 13:1–7. Record all you learn about love and pray for God to give you a heart of love for even the most difficult person in your life.

Observation

FOCUSing on Philippians 4:1–3

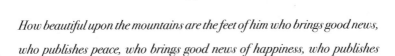

How beautiful upon the mountains are the feet of him who brings good news, who publishes peace, who brings good news of happiness, who publishes salvation. —Isaiah 52:7

WHEN WE'RE TALKING about relationships, it's important to pay attention to who we're in disagreement with. Just as I treat a two year old differently than a 42 year old, so I must learn to take a step back and take into consideration who it is I am in conflict with. Is this person a regenerate believer in the God of the Bible, or are they without the hope of Christ in their life? Are they an immature believer, or have they walked with God for decades? The biblical principles we'll look at this week are certainly helpful in most situations, but it is key for us to manage our expectations when it comes to the responses of others.

First off, we must be careful not to place biblical expectations on a person who does not know Jesus. There is no reason for me to expect someone who is not in relationship with Christ to act like Christ. Jesus was humble, full of grace, and forever loving. I've been walking with Jesus for two decades now, and I still fall short of this standard every day. Why on earth would I expect someone who does not hold a biblical worldview to act according to what I believe is right? The exhortations we'll see in these verses fall primarily to the Christian. The nonbeliever would certainly bene-fit from following a biblical model through disagreements, but we cannot expect them to do so. And so, I must manage my expecta-tions, especially with those who don't know Jesus. Because, if their heart hasn't yet been radically changed by God—like mine has—I should not expect them to take the first step toward reconciliation, to forgive unconditionally, or to act anything in line with the character of Christ.

Secondly, I must consider the maturity of the person I'm hav-ing trouble with. Are they new in Christ? Are they Christian in name only, showing very little fruit of transformation? Might they be going through a tough time at home or work? What was their upbringing like? Was Christlike behavior modeled to them? When I take a step back and ask God to allow me to see them through His eyes, it is easier to follow the example of Christ to humble myself, give abun-dant grace, and love unconditionally.

1. Ask the Holy Spirit to guide you today as you study the Word. Declare your intent to listen to His voice and obey His prompting

Look at the Details

2. Read Philippians 4:1–3 again, and look for all the commands Paul gives. Write them out below as you find them. (Check out the cheat sheet at the end of today's study if you get stuck.)

3. Which of these commands stands out to you most? Why?

4. Now read Philippians 4:1-3 yet again. Be on the lookout for descriptive truths about the individuals Paul addressed. Fill in the chart below.

Descriptive Truths about "My Brothers"
(the audience Paul was writing to)

Descriptive Truths about Euodia and Syntyche

5. Look back to the three commands given in these verses. For each, circle which group of people to whom the imperative was given.

stand firm in the Lord...	the church at Philippi	Euodia and Syntyche
agree in the Lord...	the church at Philippi *or*	Euodia and Syntyche
help these women...	the church at Philippi	Euodia and Syntyche

As I look back on these last 20 years of growth in Christ, I'm in awe of God's work in me. I also cringe when certain scenes of my past are brought to mind. Again and again, I was on the receiving end of grace after grace from friends, roommates, disciples, and parents. I've been the annoying one. I've been the selfish one. (Often, I still am. Just ask my husband and kids.) And without the restraining hand of God's grace in my life, I most certainly would still be the spotlight stealer, people bulldozer, and frenemy backstabber. *But, God.* He intervened and provided a new trajectory for my life, showing me grace again and again—oftentimes through people. From the roommates who didn't kick me out though I was hard to live with, to the friends who listened to what was on my heart again and again and again, though I never asked about their day. And now through my husband and children who choose to love and forgive me, though I mistreat and neglect them at times.

Because of His great love for me, Christ died for my sin, rescued me from death, and gave me a new, eternal life. But that's not the end of the story. God chooses to keep me on this earth; not to enjoy the comforts this life has to offer or to make myself into someone important. I exist to bring God glory. Each breath I take is a gift from God and is meant to be used for His purposes: to rescue those who have yet to enter into a relationship with Him. Therefore, when I get bogged down in the muck of a disagreement, I need to take a step back and see how this situation can be used to point others (both those within the disagreement and the bystanders looking on) to a loving, gracious God whose desire is to bring us all to a deeper place with Him.

> *{God, navigating the waters of dissent is tricky. I am desperate for Your wisdom, guidance, and grace as I strive to find unity with those I disagree with. As I see others in a disagreement, remind and enable me to point them to You and Your heart for our everyday living.}*

Bonus Study

Read Philippians 2:3–8 and make a list of all that is true of Christ. Next, look for the command in this passage and write it out. How might taking on this attitude help in the midst of a relational rift? Pray and ask God to enable you!

Cheat Sheet

2. Read Philippians 4:1–3 again, and look for all the commands Paul gives. Write them out below as you find them.

stand firm in the Lord (v. 1)

agree in the Lord (v. 2)

help these women (v. 3)

4. Now read Philippians 4:1–3 yet again. Be on the lookout for descriptive truths about the individuals Paul addressed. Fill in the chart below.

Descriptive Truths about "My Brothers" (the audience Paul was writing to)	Descriptive Truths about Euodia and Syntyche
Paul loves them Paul longs for them They are Paul's joy They are Paul's crown "My beloved" Paul addressed one as a true companion	Women Had both labored for the gospel "side by side" with Paul and other workers Their names are in the book of life. (They were true believers in Christ.)

Clarification

FOCUSing on Philippians 4:1−3

I therefore, a prisoner for the Lord, urge you to walk in a manner worthy of the calling to which you have been called, with all humility and gentleness, with patience, bearing with one another in love, eager to maintain the unity of the Spirit in the bond of peace. —Ephesians 4:1–3

AS I MENTIONED in the introduction, the minute I started writing this Bible study, God provided ample opportunity for me to practice what I preach. Typically, I do my best work in crunch time, so I like to lead a test-group study as I write a study. This provides me with a weekly deadline, and having a sweet, gracious group of women (whom I lovingly call my guinea pigs) awaiting each week's study keeps me moving forward. As I crafted this week's study, I found myself in a Christian women's group filled with the type of drama that brought back memories from junior high. Oh, my goodness. It was a mess. And, I gotta be honest, the command to "agree in the Lord" was difficult to navigate.

What exactly does it look like to "agree in the Lord" in the midst of very disagreeable people? How do I "agree in the Lord" when one moment I want to run far, far away and the next I daydream of slapping some sense into them all? (I guess I vacillate between being a fleer and a fighter!) Today we'll pick up a few of these words and inspect them more closely. As we do, I pray God will enlighten the eyes of your heart to see the truth these verses hold for the rocky relational roads ahead.

1. Continue the work of prayer, asking God to point out the areas of your heart that are hard toward others and steeped in disunity. Submit your desires and will to God's plan for your every moment.

Uncover the Original Meaning

Spend some time today discovering the original language. I've given a few suggestions of what to study but, as always, feel free to follow your own inclinations of which word to look up. If the Greek is overwhelming, simply choose a few words to look up in the dictionary and write out their definitions.

DECIDE which word you would like to study.

2. Look for any potential keywords in Philippians 4:1–3. As you find any repeated word or words that might be important to the passage, write them below.

DISCOVER that word as it was originally written.

3. Together, let's focus on the word *agree* today. Using an interlinear Bible, find the original word for *agree* used in verse 2 and write it below. Your version might use the words "have the same mind" or "live in harmony."

AGREE =

DEFINE that word.

4. Now, look up the Greek word you've uncovered using your favorite Greek study tool and try to fill out the chart on your own this time.

Greek word: _____

Verse and Version: _____

Part of Speech:	Translation Notes:
(verb, noun, etc.)	*(How else is it translated? How often is this word used?)*
Strong's Concordance Number:	Definition:
Notes:	

5. Follow the above steps to look up at least one more word. Here are a few words to choose from:

STAND FIRM (v. 1)

HELP (v. 3)

Greek word: Verse and Version:

_____   _____

Part of Speech:	Translation Notes:
(verb, noun, etc.)	(How else is it translated? How often is this word used?)
Strong's Concordance Number:	Definition:
Notes:	

6. What discoveries did you make through your Clarification study? Which word did you learn the most about?

We don't know all the ins and outs of the situation here in Philippians, but we do know there was conflict between two women (imagine that!) and it went down within a larger body of believers, the church at Philippi. So, what can we learn about how to agree in the middle of great disagreements? The encouragement here from Paul has to do with what our mind is set on. It's not a command to find a way to get along, or even to find "middle ground." To agree in the Lord is for both parties to take on the mindset of the Lord—the attitude of Christ. But when emotions rise and words start flying, my mind is not naturally set on the Lord. Instead, I'm fixed on my rights, my preferences, and my wounded heart. And, so, I must set my mind toward the example of Christ. Arguments move toward agreement when my heart is humble instead of proud, when my mindset shifts to mercy and away from allegations, and when I relinquish my rights instead of clenching my fists to fight.

Sometimes I find myself smack dab in the middle of a firestorm. Other times, I'm on the sidelines watching the destruction unfold. It's important to note: Paul's encouragement and exhortation was not just to "these women." It was also to those around them, and to them he said, "help these women." Even if we are not an active player in the conflict, we must choose to be a helpful spectator. The word for *help* in Philippians 4:3 is also translated in other passages as "impregnate" or "conceive." It gives the idea of helping the birth of something. So, then, I must ask myself: When I walk alongside those in conflict, what do I interject? What do I help to conceive in a stressful situation? It is all-too-easy to interject negative and selfish thoughts. From, "I can't believe she did that!" to "You deserve better, get rid of him!" Every statement I make to someone in conflict has the potential to birth offerings of mercy or stones of strife.

Let's point those in the middle of conflict toward the way of peace; let's attempt to quench quarrels, instead of adding fuel to the fire.

{Lord, show me what it looks like to "agree in the Lord" in my specific and difficult situations. Help me to guard my heart from bitterness and my tongue from gossip. As I see others in disagreement, help me to inject an eternal and positive perspective into the situation. In all things, make me firm in your love for me and acceptance of me.}

Bonus Study

Look up additional Greek words from our passage.

Cheat Sheet

Greek word:

PHRONEŌ

Verse and Version:

PHILIPPIANS 4:2 ESV

Part of Speech:	Translation Notes:
(verb, noun, etc.)	(How else is it translated? How often is this word used?)
verb	think (5), regard (4), mind (3), be minded (3), savour (2), be of the same mind (2), be like minded (2)

Strong's Concordance Number:	Definition:
# 5426	think; be wise

Notes:

"have attitude; ponder; hold a view; honor; be haughty"; "to be of the same mind ie agreed together, cherish the same views, be harmonious. to direct one's mind to a thing, to seek, to strive for."

Utilization

FOCUSing on Philippians 4:1−3

↠ *If possible, so far as it depends on you, live peaceably with all.* —Romans 12:18 ↞

I HAVE THREE firstborn children. No, I do not have triplets, but I do have three stubborn, strong-willed, bossy-pants kids. They get these traits honestly (from the Queen of Firstborns, yours truly), and though I know these traits can be shaped into incredible qualities of admirable persistence, strong leadership, and needed decisiveness, it disrupts the rhythms of typical birth order. It also makes for many an argument in the Orr household. Most of the time, it is because one, two, or (typically) all three of my children feel out of control. They lack the ability to bend the wills and change the minds of their siblings, and so the daily frustration ensues.

I get it. That frustration stemming from feeling completely exasperated and out of control. And, when I attempt to enter into the chaos with the example of Christ in mind, pursue peace with all I have, and I still can't control the other soul in the equation? Well, it's just plain defeating. Thankfully, I am not judged on the outcome of the fight. I am simply challenged to take control of my own actions and attitudes, and cling to the Christ who willingly walked to the Cross for me, providing an example of how to usher peace into the equation.

1. Spend some time today in praise for the relationships God has given you. Instead of focusing on the negative and discouraging, choose to dwell on the positive and encouraging.

Discover the Connections

2. Read Philippians 4:1–3 again to start your study today.

3. Look up the following cross-references that teach us more about how we are to agree in the Lord.

Philippians 2:1–2

Philippians 2:5

Romans 12:16,18

2 Corinthians 13:11

Romans 14:19

Over a decade ago, as a young believer, in the middle of massive relational turmoil with a friend, I confided in a mentor about my problems. I was torn. Pursuing peace was on my heart, but there was also a large part of me that wanted to prove my point. Reconciliation was an ideal solution . . . as long as I didn't have to be in the same room with that person again. Wise words from a woman who'd been there before brought realism and comfort to my torn and tattered soul: "Forgiveness doesn't mean everything has to go back to the way it was. You may not be able to be in the same room with them without pain for a very long time. All you can control is your heart and your actions. Let God work out the rest in His time."

My expectations for what peace in a disagreement should look like were off. I desperately needed to hear the truth she had to give, and those words have come back to me again and again over the years. Because, even on my best peace-pursuing day, there is no guarantee others will follow suit. I can only control one side of the relationship. My mind. My heart. My actions. That's a hard enough job on its own. Any fight I find myself in is less about the details of the disagreement, and all about my faithfulness to the Father. "If possible, so far as it depends on you, live peaceably with all" *(Romans 12:18).*

> *{God, I want my interactions with others to glorify You. Help me as I learn to walk in unity and agreement with all for Your name's sake.}*

Bonus Study

Look up any additional cross-references in Philippians 4:1–3 that you would like to learn more about.

Summation

FOCUSing on Philippians 4:1–3

Do nothing from selfish ambition or conceit, but in humility count others more significant than yourselves. Let each of you look not only to his own interests, but also to the interests of others. —Philippians 2:3

HUMILITY. NOT MY favorite word. Probably not yours, either. However, it truly ought to be. Without humility, you and I are doomed. Not because of the problems conceit brings into our relationships or the sure-to-fall path pride leads us into—although both of those are true. We should rejoice in humility because it has led to the greatest gift we ever received.

Without the humility of Christ, there would be no sacrifice at the Cross.

And without the mercy and redemption of the Cross of Christ, there would be no sin remedy, allowing for a relationship recovery.

And without the recovery of mankind's relationship with Christ, there is a doomed eternity.

Every soul lives on for eternity—either with or without the presence of God. And so, with eternity in mind (especially of those who do not know Jesus), I must point my heart toward the example of Christ. Because the model of Jesus is the provision of God for my every trouble, trial, and squabble.

Respond to God's Word

IDENTIFY—Find the main idea of the passage.

1. Take a few moments to flip back to each day's study to review what you've learned this week.

2. In the space below, write out Philippians 4:1–3 in your own words. Or simply write out what you think the main idea of this passage is, especially in regards to our study of peace.

3. Read a commentary or study Bible to see how your observations from this week line up with the scholars. As you search the commentaries, ask God to make clear the meaning of any passages that are fuzzy to you. Record any additional observations below.

MODIFY—Evaluate my beliefs in light of the main idea.

Prayerfully journal through the following questions, asking for the Spirit of God to enlighten and convict you.

4. Are most of your relationships characterized by dissension or unity? Have you done everything possible to keep peace with the individuals in your life?

5. Write down the name of one person with whom you are currently experiencing frustration. How can you obey the command to "agree in the Lord" with this person?

6. Are you more concerned with making your point or agreeing in the Lord? Does the peace of God rule your heart or selfishness, rivalry, and pride? What are you standing firm in? Your own will and selfish desire or the Lord's plan and provision for you?

7. When you walk alongside those in conflict, what do you tend to interject into the situation?

GLORIFY—Align my life to reflect the truth of God's Word.

8. What adjustments can you make this week to move toward peace in your relationships?

9. Pick one adjustment and write it down below. Ask God to help you as you move toward this person in unity and love.

Peace with people is a lofty goal indeed. But only if we pursue it on our own. Peace comes from God alone. It's His gift to provide. The part we play is to follow hard after Him and the example He left us, through His Son, the Christ. We cannot do it alone, but it can be done. For the sake of God's glory, let's pursue peace.

> *{God, I invite you to illuminate my heart to the ways I can better love, serve, and count others as more significant than myself. I can follow the humble example of Christ only by Your strength and grace.}*

In Closing

We've traveled a lot of ground together. Anxiety. Discontentment. Dissension. I'll admit, I struggle with all three, and through the journey of writing this study, I am even more aware of my selfishness, my combativeness, and my forgetfulness to walk in the example of Christ. My heart is easily distracted from finding satisfaction in Christ alone, and my mind is ever swirling with lies leading me toward the way of anxiety instead of a life of peace. Yet God is faithful regardless of my tendency to wander from the peace He promises.

Together, let's commit anew to follow the example of Christ, not the world. Each morning, let's wake readied to fight for peace. Today, let's resolve again and again (and again) to trust in His character, not our wavering emotions.

By His great grace, we can stand firm in His promises for everyday peace.

Appendix

Time line of Paul's Life

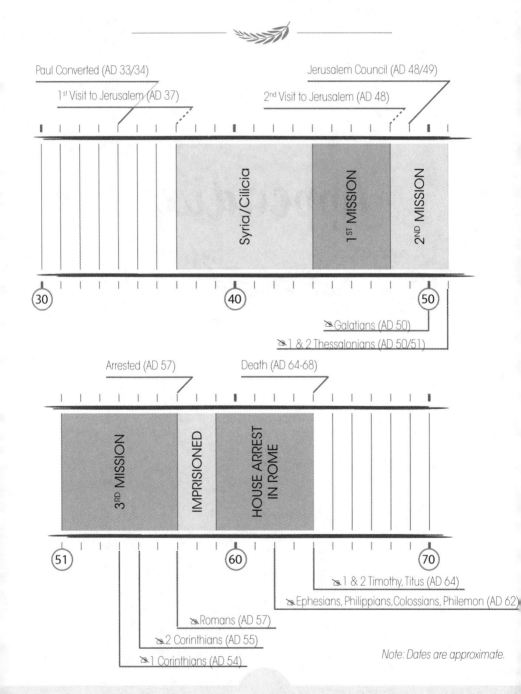

Paul Converted (AD 33/34)

Jerusalem Council (AD 48/49)

1st Visit to Jerusalem (AD 37)

2nd Visit to Jerusalem (AD 48)

Syria/Cilicia

1ST MISSION

2ND MISSION

30

40

50

Galatians (AD 50)

1 & 2 Thessalonians (AD 50/51)

Arrested (AD 57)

Death (AD 64-68)

3RD MISSION

IMPRISIONED

HOUSE ARREST IN ROME

51

60

70

1 & 2 Timothy, Titus (AD 64)

Ephesians, Philippians, Colossians, Philemon (AD 62)

Romans (AD 57)

2 Corinthians (AD 55)

1 Corinthians (AD 54)

Note: Dates are approximate.

Truths about Peace

Use this space to record all of the truths that you discover about peace.

Master Sheet

Glossary of Bible Study Terms

INTERLINEAR BIBLE: a translation where each English word is linked to its original Greek word. There are many free interlinear Bibles online, as well as great apps you can download to your phone or tablet. Check out KatieOrr.me/Resources for current links.

CONCORDANCE: a helpful list of words found in the original languages of the Bible (mainly Hebrew and Greek) and the verses where you can find them.

CROSS-REFERENCE: a notation in a Bible verse that indicates there are other passages that contain similar material.

FOOTNOTE: a numerical notation that refers readers to the bottom of a page for additional information.

COMMENTARY: a reference book written by experts that explains the Bible. A good commentary will give you historical background and language information that may not be obvious from the passage.

GREEK: the language in which most of the New Testament was written.

HEBREW: the language in which most of the Old Testament was written.

Structure and Books of the Bible

Old Testament

→ **Books of the Law (also known as the Pentateuch)**

Genesis	Numbers
Exodus	Deuteronomy
Leviticus	

→ **Books of History**

Joshua	2 Kings
Judges	1 Chronicles
Ruth	2 Chronicles
1 Samuel	Ezra
2 Samuel	Nehemiah
1 Kings	Esther

→ **Wisdom Literature**

Job	Ecclesiastes
Psalms	Song of Songs
Proverbs	

→ **Major Prophets**

Isaiah	Ezekiel
Jeremiah	Daniel
Lamentations	

→ **Minor Prophets**

Hosea	Nahum
Joel	Habakkuk
Amos	Zephaniah
Obadiah	Haggai
Jonah	Zechariah
Micah	Malachi

New Testament

→ **Narratives (First four together are known as "The Gospels")**

Matthew	John
Mark	Acts
Luke	

→ **Epistles (or Letters) by Paul**

Romans	1 Thessalonians
1 Corinthians	2 Thessalonians
2 Corinthians	1 Timothy
Galatians	2 Timothy
Ephesians	Titus
Philippians	Philemon
Colossians	

→ **General Epistles (Letters not by Paul)**

Hebrews	1 John
James	2 John
1 Peter	3 John
2 Peter	Jude

→ **Apocalyptic Writing**

Revelation

Major Themes of the Bible

Though many view Scripture as a patchwork of historical accounts, morality tales, and wisdom for daily living, the Bible is really only one story—the mind-blowing story of God's plan to rescue fallen humanity. This storyline flows through every single book, chapter, verse, and word of Scripture. It's crucial that we know the movements, or themes, of the grand storyline so we don't miss the point of the passage we are studying.

For example, I grew up hearing the story of David's adulterous affair with the beautiful, but married, Bathsheba. I heard how he covered his misdeeds with a murderous plot to snuff out her husband. This story was usually punctuated with a moral that went something like this, "Don't take what isn't yours!" While it is indeed good practice to refrain from taking what isn't ours, there is a much bigger connection to the grand story that we will miss if we stop at a moral lesson. So what then is this grand story, and how can we recognize it?

The story falls into four main themes, or movements: creation, fall, redemption, and completion*.

Creation

The Bible begins by describing the creative work of God. His master-work and crowning achievement was the creation of people. God put the first couple, Adam and Eve, in absolute paradise and gave them everything they needed to thrive. The best part of this place, the Garden of Eden, was that God walked among His people. They knew Him and were known by Him. The Bible even says they walked around naked because they had no concept of shame or guilt. (See Genesis 2:25.) Life was perfect, just like God had designed.

Fall

In the Garden, God provided everything for Adam and Eve. But He also gave them instructions for how to live and established boundaries for their protection. Eventually, the first family decided to cross a boundary and break the one rule God commanded them to keep. This decision was the most fateful error in history. At that precise moment, paradise was lost. The connection that people experienced with God vanished. Adam and Eve's act was not simply a mistake but outright rebellion against the sovereign Creator of the universe. It was, in no uncertain terms, a declaration of war against God. Every aspect of creation was fractured in that moment. Because of their choice, Adam and Eve introduced death and disease to the world, but more importantly, put a chasm between mankind and God that neither Adam nor Eve nor any person could ever hope to cross. Ever since the fall, all people are born with a tendency to sin. Like moths to a light, we are drawn to sin, and like Adam and Eve, our sin pushes us further away from any hope of experiencing God. You see God cannot be good if He doesn't punish sin, but if we all receive the punishment our sin deserves we would all be cast away from Him forever.

Redemption

Fortunately, God was not caught off guard when Adam and Eve rebelled. God knew they would and had a plan in place to fix what they had broken. This plan meant sending Jesus to earth. Even though Jesus was the rightful King of all creation, He came to earth in perfect humility. He walked the earth for more than 30 years experiencing everything you and I do. Jesus grew tired at the end of a long day. He got hungry when He didn't eat. He felt the pain of losing loved ones, and the disappointment of betrayal from friends. He went through all of life like we do with one mas-sive exception—He never sinned. Jesus never disobeyed God, not even once. Because He was without sin, He was the only one in history who could bridge the gap between God and us. How-ever, redemption came at a steep price. Jesus was nailed to a wooden cross and left to die a criminal's death. While He hung on the Cross, God put the full weight of our sin upon Jesus. When the King of the universe died, He paid the penalty for our sin. God poured out His righteous anger toward our sin on the sinless One. After Jesus died, He was buried and many believed all hope was lost. However, Jesus did not stay dead—having defeated sin on the Cross, He was raised from death and is alive today!

Completion

The final theme in the grand storyline of the Bible is completion, the end of the story. Now that Jesus has paid the penalty for our sin, we have hope of reconciliation with God. This is such tremendous news because reconciliation means we are forgiven of sin and given eternal life. Reconciliation means that God dwells with us again. Finally, we know Him and are known by Him. Completion for us means entering into reconciliation with God through the only means He provided. We can only experience reconciliation under God's rescue plan if we trust Jesus to pay for our sin and demonstrate this by repenting, or turning away, from our sin. But God's rescue plan does not end with us. One day, Jesus will come back and ultimately fix every part of fallen creation. King Jesus will come back to rule over God's people, and again establish a paradise that is free from the effects of sin.

Let's return to the David and Bathsheba story for a moment and try to find our place. David was the greatest, most godly king in the history of the Old Testament, but even he was affected by the fall and had a sinful nature. This story points out that what we really need is not a more disciplined eye, but a total transformation. We need to be delivered from the effects of the fall. It also illustrates how we don't simply need a king who loves God, but we need a King who is God. Do you see how this story connects to the arc of the grand storyline? Just look at how much glorious truth we miss out on if we stop short at "don't take what isn't yours."

For a more detailed discussion on these themes, refer to Part 1 and 2 of The Explicit Gospel *by Matt Chandler (pages 21–175) or Chapter 2 of Mark Dever's* The Gospel and Personal Evangelism *(pages 31–44).*

How to Do a Greek/Hebrew Word Study

Learning more about the language used in the original version of Scripture can be a helpful tool toward a better understanding of the author's original meaning and intention in writing. The Old Testament was written in Hebrew and the New Testament in Greek. Though the thought of learning a new language is overwhelming to most of us, we live in an age with incredible tools at our fingertips through smartphone apps and online websites (many of which are free!), which make understanding the original meaning as simple as looking a word up in a dictionary.

Here are three easy steps to work toward a better understanding of the verses you study.

DECIDE which word you would like to study.

Do a quick read of your passage and note any potential keywords and/or repeated words. There is no right or wrong way to do this! Simply select a few words you would like to learn more about.

DISCOVER that word as it was originally written.

Using an interlinear Bible *(see glossary)*, find the original Greek (if New Testament) or Hebrew (if Old Testament) word for each instance of the word in the passage you are studying. There may be more than one Greek or Hebrew word present that translated into one English word.

DEFINE that word.

Look up your Greek/Hebrew word (or words if you found more than one) in a Greek/Hebrew lexicon. Most of the free apps and websites available do this with a simple click of a button, opening up a wealth of information referenced from a lexicon they've chosen. I encourage you to check out the videos I've created to show you how to use many of the online Greek tools. You can find them at KatieOrr.me/Resources.

Though this step can seem overwhelming, once you find an app or site you love, it is as simple as looking up a word in the dictionary. Here is a chart you can use to record what you learn.

Greek/Hebrew Word Study Worksheet

Greek word: **Verse and Version:**

_____   _____

Part of Speech:	Translation Notes:
(verb, noun, etc.)	(How else is it translated? How often is this word used?)
Strong's Concordance Number:	**Definition:**
Notes:	

How to Do a Greek/Hebrew Word Study—Example

Let's walk through this process, looking at Hebrews 11:1 together. I've also included extra notes to help you better understand the behind-the-scenes work the apps and websites are doing for us.

DECIDE which word you would like to study.

Since Hebrews is in the New Testament, we'll be working with the Greek language. To start your Greek study, look for any potential keywords in Hebrews 11:1. As you find any repeated word or words that seem important to the passage, write them down.

faith, assurance, hoped, conviction, things, seen

Since faith is probably what the main point of this verse is about, let's study this word together.

DISCOVER that word as it was originally written.

Now that we know what we want to study, we can look up the English word *faith* in an interlinear Bible to find out what the original Greek word is. An interlinear Bible will show you English verses and line up each word next to the Greek words they were translated from. If you own or have seen a parallel Bible, with two or more English translation versions (ie, ESV, KJV, NIV) lined up next to each other, this is the same concept. Interlinear Bibles have the original language alongside an English translation.

Let's take the first phrase in Hebrews 11:1 to see how this works:

Now faith is the assurance of things hoped for. —*Hebrews 11:1*

In Greek, it looks like this: ἔστιν δὲ πίστις ἐλπιζομένων.

Most people (including me!) can't read this, so the transliteration of the Greek is often provided for us as well. This transliteration is simply the sound of each Greek letter turned into English letters to spell out how the Greek is read. It's a phonetic spelling of the Greek word. For example, the first Greek words we see, *ἔστιν* and *δὲ* are transliterated into *estin* and *de,* which is how they are pronounced.

The interlinear Bible simply lines up the two versions (and typically the transliteration as well) so we can see which word goes with which, like this:

ἔστιν	δὲ	πίστις	ἐλπιζομένων
estin	de	pistis	elpizomenōn
is	now	faith	of things hoped for

Now you can use this layout to find the original word for faith. Do you see it?

Faith=pistis=πίστις

DEFINE that word.

Now that we know the original word for faith used in Hebrews 11:1 is *pistis,* we can look up that Greek word in a Greek lexicon (which is like a dictionary) and note what we learn about the original meaning of the word. I've provided a worksheet to record this info. *(For a free printable version of this worksheet, go to KatieOrr.me /Resources and look for the PRINTABLES section.)*

Greek word:

__PISTIS__

Verse and Version:

__HEBREWS 11:1 ESV__

Part of Speech:	Translation Notes:
(verb, noun, etc.)	(How else is it translated? How often is this word used?)
noun	Used 243 times in the New Testament ESV. All but two times it is translated "faith." Other two translations: assurance (1) and belief (1)

Strong's Concordance Number:	Definition:
#G4102	faith, confidence, fidelity, guarantee, loyalty

Notes:

"pistis, which derives from peithomai ('be persuaded, have confidence, obey'), connotes persuasion, conviction, and commitment, and always implies confidence, which is expressed in human relationships as fidelity, trust, assurance, oath, proof, guarantee. Only this richness of meaning can account for the faith (pistei, kata pistin, dia pisteōs) that inspired the conduct of the great Israelite ancestors of Hebrews 11."

The Good News

God Loves You

You are known and deeply loved by a great, glorious, and personal God. This God hand-formed you for a purpose *(Ephesians 2:10)*, He has called you by name *(Isaiah 43:1)*, and you are of great worth to Him *(Luke 12:6–7)*.

We Have a Sin Problem

We are all sinners and are all therefore separated from God *(Romans 3:23; 6:23)*. Even the "smallest" of sins is a great offense to God. He is a righteous judge who will not be in the presence of sin and cannot allow sin to go unpunished. Our natural tendency toward sin has left us in desperate need of rescue because God must deal with our sin.

Jesus Is the Only Solution

Since God's standard is perfection, and we have all fallen short of the mark, Jesus is the only answer to our sin problem *(John 14:6)*. Jesus lived a life of perfect obedience to God. So when Jesus died on the Cross, He alone was able to pay the penalty of our sin.

After His death, Jesus rose from the dead, defeating death, and providing the one way we could be reconciled to God *(2 Corinthians 5:17–21)*. Jesus Christ is the only one who can save us from our sins.

We Must Choose to Believe

Trusting Christ is our only part in the gospel. Specifically, the Bible requires us to have faith in what Christ has done on our behalf *(Ephesians 2:8–9)*. This type of faith is not just belief in God. Many people grow up believing that God exists but never enter into the Christian faith. Faith that saves comes from a desperate heart. A heart that longs for Jesus—the only solution for their sin problem—to be first and foremost in their life. We demonstrate that we have this type of saving faith by turning away, or repenting, from our sin.

FOCUSed 15 Study Method

Apply this method to 2–10 verses a day, over a week's time, for a deep encounter with God through His Word, in as little as 15 minutes a day.

Foundation: Enjoy Every Word

Read and rewrite the passage—summarize, draw pictures, sentence-diagram, or simply copy the passage. Do whatever helps you slow down and enjoy each word.

Observation: Look at the Details

Take notes on what you see—write down truths in this passage. Look for truths about the character of God, promises to cling to, or commands given.

Clarification: Uncover the Original Meaning

→ **Decide which word you would like to study.**
   Look for any repeated words or keywords to look up, choose one, and learn more about it.

» **Discover that word as it was originally written.**
Using an interlinear Bible, find the original Greek or
Hebrew word for the English word you chose.

» **Define that word.**
Learn the full meaning of the word using a Greek or
Hebrew lexicon, which is very much like a dictionary.

Utilization: Discover the Connections

Cross-reference—Look up the references in each verse to view the
threads and themes throughout the Bible.

Summation: Respond to God's Word

» **Identify—Find the main idea of the passage.**

» **Modify—Evaluate my beliefs in light of the main idea.**

» **Glorify—Align my life to reflect the truth of God's Word.**

New Hope® Publishers is a division of WMU®, an international organization that challenges Christian believers to understand and be radically involved in God's mission. For more information about WMU, go to wmu.com. More information about New Hope books may be found at **NewHopePublishers.com**. New Hope books may be purchased at your local bookstore.

If you've been blessed by this book, we would like to hear your story. The publisher and author welcome your comments and suggestions at:

NEWHOPEREADER@WMU.ORG.

Use the QR reader on your smartphone to visit us online at **NewHopePublishers.com**.